The UEFA European Football Championships

This book explores social and political issues and trends emerging around the UEFA European Football Championships. It presents a contemporary sociology of the European Championships which, despite its significance as a mega-event, has been largely overshadowed by the Olympics and the FIFA World Cup in existing literature.

At a time when both sport mega-events and Europe are undergoing dramatic transformations, this book explores a range of case studies and important topics such as changing consumption patterns, new types of sport media, social media, environmental policies and emergency politics, public opposition and co-hosting. It also situates the European Championships within wider European projects and discourses of European identities, integration and enlargement. Drawing on data from recent and historical European Championships, and looking ahead to the next tournament in Germany in 2024, this book serves to open up new debates within the sociology of sport and the study of mega-events.

It is a timely and ground-breaking text which will resonate with students, academics and readers who are interested in football, the sociology of sport, mega-events, digital sociology, European politics and culture or sports business.

Jan Andre Lee Ludvigsen is Senior Lecturer in International Relations and Politics with Sociology at Liverpool John Moores University, UK. His research field is in the political sociology of sport and his research on mega-events, security, globalization, risk and fandom has been published in internationally leading journals including the *International Review for the Sociology of Sport*, *Journal of Consumer Culture*, *Leisure Studies* and *Journal of Sport and Social Issues*.

Renan Petersen-Wagner is Senior Lecturer in Sport Business and Marketing at Leeds Beckett University, UK. His research interests are within the broad field of media studies in sport, but particularly concerned with the current platformization of society. Renan's research on fandom, cosmopolitanism, mediatization, the Global South and disability sport has been published in journals including *Current Sociology*, *Journal of Sport and Social Issues*, *International Review for the Sociology of Sport*, and *Sport in Society*.

Critical Research in Football

Series Editors:
Pete Millward, *Liverpool John Moores University, UK*
Jamie Cleland, *University of Southern Australia*
Dan Parnell, *University of Liverpool, UK*
Stacey Pope, *Durham University, UK*
Paul Widdop, *Manchester Metropolitan University, UK*

The *Critical Research in Football* book series was launched in 2017 to showcase the inter- and multi-disciplinary breadth of debate relating to 'football'. The series defines 'football' as broader than association football, with research on rugby, Gaelic and gridiron codes also featured. Including monographs, edited collections, short books and textbooks, books in the series are written and/or edited by leading experts in the field whilst consciously also affording space to emerging voices in the area, and are designed to appeal to students, postgraduate students and scholars who are interested in the range of disciplines in which critical research in football connects. The series is published in association with the *Football Collective*, @FB_Collective.

Available in this series:

For more information about this series, please visit:www.routledge.com/Critical-Research-in-Football/book-series/CFSFC

The UEFA European Football Championships

Politics, Media Spectacle and
Social Change

**Jan Andre Lee Ludvigsen and
Renan Petersen-Wagner**

Routledge
Taylor & Francis Group

LONDON AND NEW YORK

First published 2023
by Routledge
4 Park Square, Milton Park, Abingdon, Oxon OX14 4RN

and by Routledge
605 Third Avenue, New York, NY 10158

Routledge is an imprint of the Taylor & Francis Group, an informa business

British Library Cataloguing-in-Publication Data
A catalogue record for this book is available from the British Library

Library of Congress Cataloging-in-Publication Data
Names: Ludvigsen, Jan Andre Lee, author. | Petersen-Wagner, Renan,
    author.
Title: The UEFA European football championships : politics, media
    spectacle and social change / Jan Andre Lee Ludvigsen and Renan
    Petersen-Wagner.
Description: Abingdon, Oxon ; New York, N.Y. : Routledge, 2023. | Series:
    Critical research in football | Includes bibliographical references and
    index.
Identifiers: LCCN 2022041970 | ISBN 9781032416489 (hardback) |
    ISBN 9781032416519 (paperback) | ISBN 9781003359098 (ebook)
Subjects: LCSH: European Championship (Soccer tournament) | Soccer—
    Social aspects—Europe. | Soccer—Press coverage—Europe. | Mass
    media and sports—Europe. | Social change—Europe. | Europe—Social
    conditions—21st century.
Classification: LCC GV943.52 .L84 2023 | DDC 796.334094—dc23/
    eng/20220930
LC record available at https://lccn.loc.gov/2022041970

ISBN: 978-1-032-41648-9 (hbk)
ISBN: 978-1-032-41651-9 (pbk)
ISBN: 978-1-003-35909-8 (ebk)

DOI: 10.4324/9781003359098

Typeset in Times New Roman
by Apex CoVantage, LLC

Contents

List of Figures

List of Tables

Acknowledgements

We would first like to collectively thank Simon Whitmore at Routledge for his support, positivity, and feedback which we always highly appreciate, and which have benefited this book. Similarly, we are thankful for the editorial support and guidance provided by Rebecca Connor at Routledge.

We also offer an enormous thank-you to Peter Millward. Peter deserves a special acknowledgement, not only as the Series Editor of this book series, but as a person whose support and guidance over the years have shaped our thinking. Thanks also to the anonymous reviewers who provided valuable comments during the proposal stage of this book.

Renan wants to thank all his colleagues at Leeds Beckett University, especially Alex Bond and Francesco Addesa for all their methodological and theoretical support in previous and current research projects that ultimately shaped some of the ideas present in this book. Renan wants also to acknowledge all the students in the different modules he leads – Digital Business, Sport Broadcasting, Digital Media for International Marketing, Media and Digital Transformations – for all the invaluable discussions and insights during seminars and workshops. Jan deserves a special thanks for his friendship and chats over social media that provide a constant influx of new ideas, which ultimately serve as a reminder of what a true research partnership is. Finally, Renan wants to thank his parents and siblings for all their unconditional support over the years.

Jan wishes to express his gratitude to his colleagues at LJMU's departments of International Relations & Politics and Sociology. In no particular order, he would also like to thank Mark Turner, David Webber, Dan Feather, Jack Sugden, Joe Moran, Seamus Byrne, John Hayton and Dan Parnell for always taking time to listen to and shape his ideas, and for providing feedback and support. Of course, he also thanks his co-author, Renan, for friendship, support and his outstanding enthusiasm on this and other research projects which have been a genuine privilege to work on together over the last years. Jan also wants to thank Zelda, Jodie and his family for their constant support, love and patience over the years.

Finally, it is necessary to acknowledge that any potential errors in this book are entirely those of the authors.

1 Introduction

The European festival

This book advances a contemporary sociological understanding of the Union of European Football Associations (UEFA) European Championships in football (popularly known and referred to as the 'Euros'). It does so by focusing on emerging social and political issues and trends within this mega-event's context, hence extending relevant academic debates (King, 2003, 2010; Levermore and Millward, 2007; Millward, 2010; Manzenreiter and Spitaler, 2010) and arguing that the Euros are a key driver and expression for social change. As contended, by analysing the European Championships, it is possible to understand a set of broader issues within European politics, cultures and societies, as well as developments situated within the dynamic universe of sport mega-events speaking to digitalization, mediatization practices, event bidding and hosting and emergency politics in the twenty-first century (Horne, 2010; Roche, 2017). The book's key argument carries a special significance when considering the European Championship's role as a European festival, one of the largest and most important mega-events in the world, and how the tournament cuts across European popular and consumer culture, urban spaces and political and economic fields.

The social history of the Euros is one of enlargement, transformation and social change. Since it was first staged in France in 1960 – with merely four competing nations playing games across two host cities – the Euros (then named the 'European Nations Cup') have become increasingly prestigious and expanded substantially in its scale. Consequently, a myriad of sociological issues has emerged *within* or *from* the event that is staged in four-year cycles (Millward, 2010). As we write this, the most recent men's European Championships (the postponed 2020 edition staged in 2021) took place with 24 qualified nations across no fewer than 11 different European countries – with extremely varying Covid-19 and travelling restrictions – during the pandemic (Lee Ludvigsen, 2022a). Although this edition's continent-wide style represented an exception with respect to its hosting format, it

DOI: 10.4324/9781003359098-1

accurately illustrated not solely the sheer *size* of this mega-event, but how it is deeply entangled in European and world politics and influenced by interactions between states, international organizations and non-state actors (Lee Ludvigsen, 2022b). The present-day Championship is also embedded in broader consumer cultures. Many fans and consumers physically attend stadiums and fan zones. Others, meanwhile, consume the Euros digitally on television or 'new media' platforms, including YouTube, Twitter (Chapters 3 and 4), Instagram and TikTok, which have become significant spaces where football-related moments and socio-political issues are discussed, shared and reacted to globally (UEFA, n.d.).

Both before, and especially after the 'pandemic summer' of 2021, socially and politically intriguing questions have continued to emerge in relation to the Euros. Some of these include speculations that the tournament could expand further to 32 competing countries (translating to more fixtures and potentially more revenue),[1] calls for Ukraine to host Euro 2028 following the Russian invasion in 2022, and a planned joint Irish and UK bid for the same event (*The Guardian*, 2022; Chapter 5). All this underpins why there have been efforts made by scholars to consistently 'demonstrate the close connection between European football and the wider political and social order' (King, 2010: 890). As central to this book, it can be argued that pressing sociological and political questions are omnipresent in the tournament's spheres. As we return to later, several of these questions will be addressed over the course of this book.

The importance of this book and its arguments speak to how they capture a mega-event that, despite some attention, has been left somewhat under-researched. For instance, to date, and within the distinct (but often intersecting) fields of European studies, critical football studies and sport mega-event studies, only a limited number of scholarly books have critically and directly engaged with the European Championships despite its position as the third-largest sport mega-event in the world. Whilst we return to and unpack the 'Euro-specific' literature in more depth in Chapter 2, existing texts include Alpan et al.'s (2015) edited collection with chapters focused on mediatization, identities and fandom (predominantly) at Euro 2008 and 2012. Moreover, the special issue of *Soccer & Society* (Volume 11, Issue 6) – edited by Manzenreiter and Spitaler (2010) – also represents a comprehensive volume with contributions addressing the tournament's political economy and attempts to look into what the future holds for the European football more broadly in 'new Europe' (King, 2010). As the guest editors wrote, their ambition for their special issue was to:

> demonstrate . . . what separates the new European Football Championships from earlier stages of European football is exactly the new

centrality of European sport mega-events for questions of governance, citizenship and Europeanization.

(Manzenreiter and Spitaler, 2010: 704)

Notwithstanding, whilst this special issue successfully does that, this also implies that the European Championships is constantly evolving. And, in a way, this calls for a revisitation of the Euros. Thus, although there has been important work published on diverse topics (Klauser, 2017; Lee Ludvigsen, 2020, 2021, 2022a, 2022b; Włoch, 2013; Chapter 2) following Mittag and Legrand's (2010: 710) argument that 'the need for more in-depth studies on European-oriented football is apparent', it could be argued that this call still can be echoed in the early 2020s. More recently, in *Sport Mega-Events, Security and Covid-19*, Lee Ludvigsen (2022a) focused specifically on the exceptional case study of Euro 2020 and critically examined its 'security' and Covid-related disruptions. In short, the mentioned book argues that European Championships in football express and reflect wider security-oriented trends in modern societies. Yet due to the monograph's scope, some of the wider sociological questions associated with the Euros, such as its relationship to digitalization processes, environment politics, bidding processes and mediation practices – some of which we cover in the current book – were never engaged with in-depth. Meanwhile, O'Brien's (2021) encyclopaedic *Euro Summits: The Story of the UEFA European Championships 1960 to 2021* – whilst directed more at the general readership – provides a social history of the increasingly growing European spectacle, with chapters dedicated to each tournament in the period between 1960 and 2016.

Notwithstanding, whilst academic books on the *Fédération Internationale de Football Association* (FIFA) World Cup (Chadwick et al., 2022; Dunn, 2015; Arnold, 2021; Bandyopadhyay et al., 2018; Brannagan and Reiche, 2022) and Olympics (Boykoff, 2014, 2016, 2020; Frawley and Adair, 2013; Horne and Whannel, 2016; Goldblatt, 2016) have continued to surface at an impressive pace throughout the 2010s and early 2020s, it is fair to claim that the European Championships has received substantially less attention despite its global audience and symbolic position in the mega-event calendar and European societies (see Chapters 2, 3 and 4).

However, our aim here is not merely to give the Euros scholarly recognition *per se*. That is simply because scholars from various disciplines – including sociology (Millward, 2010; Horne, 2010; King, 2010), political science (Włoch, 2013; Lee Ludvigsen, 2022a) and urban geography (Klauser, 2017) – have already recognized the social importance of Euros, collectively supporting the notion that the 'centrality of football in European cultures and societies has been established over time by its unique position as the national sport in almost any European country' (Manzenreiter and Spitaler, 2010: 695). Rather, in the context of what is commonly characterized as a 'turbulent' time for European societies (Giddens, 2014) (amplified by, for example, Covid-19 and the 'post-pandemic' epoch, Brexit and the 2022 Russian invasion of Ukraine),[2] and the constantly changing worlds of football (Giulianotti, 1999), sport mega-events (Roche, 2017) and the sport-media landscape, it should be highlighted that this book's primary aim is to reconsider the European Championships whilst capturing and making sociological sense of the Championships' key trends over the last two decades.

The advancement further towards a current sociology of the European Championships lies at the heart of this book. Particularly, we do so by addressing diverse aspects of the Euros speaking to digitalization, mediatization, emergency and security, and the politics of event bidding and hosting. In order to achieve these aims, there are three key objectives that this book seeks to accomplish. These objectives concern themselves with both the event's *past* and *present*. Concisely summarized, they include:

- To revisit the emergence and key actors of the Euros;
- To identify pressing social issues and trends of sport and mega-events and situate these in recent Euros case studies;
- To formulate an emerging research agenda for future, sustained and inter-disciplinary work on the Euros and mega-events.

Having unpacked the key rationale and aims of this monograph, we now seek to discuss key debates surrounding two key concepts that collectively form the baseline for this book: that is, 'Europe' and 'sport mega-events'. After that, we provide some notes on our approaches and on the book's original contributions.

The meanings of Europe

As *the* main football tournament for men's national teams in Europe, the European Championships represent Europe's key sport mega-event. Beyond representing a sport and media spectacle, however, this mega-event could also be considered a celebration or expression of 'pan-Europeanism' or ideas of 'Europe' and its political project. Although the Euros' historical foundations are returned to in Chapter 2, it remains important to highlight that:

> [T]he development of the European Championship in football parallels the development of a European economic 'common market' and

political union over the past 45 years and as such also has representational implications for European identities.

(Horne, 2010: 855)

Goldblatt (2019: 236) also states that, since the turn of the century, 'European football appeared to reflect and nurture many of the best features of the continent: political, economic and cultural'. Others have suggested that Europeanization processes within the realms of politics and the economy formulate the backdrop for wider transformations within the European production and consumption of football across local, national, international and transnational settings (Manzenreiter and Spitaler, 2010). Therefore, in order to position the European Championships within the social, cultural and political contexts from which the tournament has emerged and evolved in Chapter 2, it is crucial to first engage in a brief discussion of what 'Europe' is, and second, replicate the question asked by Featherstone (2003: 3), namely: 'What does "Europeanization" mean?'.

Concerning the former, Millward (2009: 14) writes that the meanings of 'Europe' are contested and can transcend both geographical considerations and the European Union's (EU) current 27 member countries. Thus, no single or universally applied definitions of the term exist and, indeed, 'to the geographer, Europe is something different than to the historian or the politician' because definitions may be framed in terms of cultural, political or continental reference points (Manzenreiter and Spitaler, 2010: 697). Millward (2009: 14) thus suggests that:

> if a list of European nations were compiled, Norway, Switzerland, maybe even Turkey and Russia would probably be included. If the person making the list had just watched an international football match, Israel might also be included. Yet, none are EU states.

Hence, in addition to the EU member states or, indeed, the 'geographical Europe', others may consider Europe as a part of the Eurasia continental area, the territory of European Higher Education Area (Kushnir, 2016) or the European Economic Community (hereafter EEC) (Castells, 1994). Meanwhile, others contend that Europe could be understood as a socially constructed imaginary that is established through symbols or various forms of popular culture (McNeill, 2014).

Still, as Delanty (1995: 128) argues, the idea of a European identity as orchestrated through EEC could also be understood as 'pathetic exercises in cultural engineering' that were doomed to fail as its attempt to move beyond nation-state cultures borrowed the exact same elements (e.g., flag, anthem, passport) that sustained the existences of distinctive *cultures*. Furthermore, the failure to create this *European* culture resided in the fact that most of the elements that were used for legitimizing such an identity were taken from highbrow culture, whereas national cultures emerged from the popular (ibid.). Thus, examining one of the most ordinary passions – football – might provide clues through which we can understand what it means to be 'European'.

Crucially, Europe can also be defined in football terms as it is by UEFA (Millward, 2009), which owns the commercial rights to and administers the Euros and European football more widely. Interestingly, the governing body of European football describes itself as the: 'umbrella organization for 55 national football associations across Europe' (UEFA, 2019). Whilst this, in practice, means that access to and participation in the European Championships depend on status as a European football association (Horne, 2010), other membership criteria have also included recognition by (or membership in) the United Nation (UN), whilst the organization – in exceptional circumstances – has allowed for national football associations located in another continent to be admitted should they not be a member of that relevant continent's confederation (Kassimeris, 2017).

Significantly, this means that UEFA's map of Europe differs from the EU map and 'all conventional manifestations of the continent' since its member countries also include countries like Armenia, Azerbaijan, Georgia and Kazakhstan, which share borders with remote European nations (ibid.: 436). Meanwhile, Israel, which has been a full UEFA member since 1991, has also organized U21 Men's and U19 Women's Euros (UEFA, 2022). In that respect, 'Europe' possesses a unique meaning when applied to UEFA-governed football in the present day.

Concerning 'Europeanization', this concept has been much discussed since the 1990s (Borneman and Fowler, 1997; Featherstone, 2003). As a process, however, Europeanization must not be interpreted as synonymous with convergence or homogenization (Borneman and Fowler, 1997). That is because convergence is not always the end-product of Europeanization (Brand et al., 2013). First and broadly, Europeanization can refer to the 'top-down' processes relating to transformation at the domestic level in member states that are influenced by European-level institutions and structures (Ladrech, 2002), as well as ongoing projects speaking to institution building and the spread of an 'EU identity' or a European awareness (Borneman and Fowler, 1997; Mittag and Legrand, 2010).

Second, it is possible to speak of 'bottom-up' Europeanization. This refers to how national policies and domestic actors can influence or impact European-level politics (Brand et al., 2013). Moreover, another possible form of understanding Europeanization is to look at both *vertical* (top-bottom; bottom-up) and also *horizontal* processes such as education, culture, labour, identity and language (Beck and Grande, 2008). Here, we can situate football as an example of the *horizontal* Europeanization that Beck and Grande

(2008: 98) alluded to, as it provides a shared *European* social space where 'the power of nation-state borders to shape societies is diminishing'. Nevertheless, whilst Beck and Grande (2008) emphasized the everyday *horizontal* Europeanization, we remain focused in this book on an ephemeral mega-event that takes place every four years and provides a reinforcement of *doing Europe* [an identity].

How can one locate the European Championships within these wider projects? The short answer is that sport and football can be seen as playing a role within wider Europeanization processes. As King's (2003) seminal *The European Ritual* documents, football in Europe constitutes a public ritual. Through European football, King argues, networks of solidarity and capital emerge. Further, as Hänska and Bauchowitz (2019: 2) remind us, Europeanization 'appears to be event-driven [and] propelled by European events' like crises, elections or changes in the Eurozone. Whilst this speaks to the importance of shared experiences of specific reference points, Europeanization can also, as Delanty (2005) points out, be manifested through work, leisure, tourism and sport. Whereas some suggest that certain sporting and cultural events like the European Capital of Culture, Eurovision Song Contest and Ryder Cup (golf) could be occasions that normatively act as sources for Europeanization (Yair, 2019; Harris, 2018; Sassatelli, 2008), it remains important not to uncritically accept these exercises as automatically translating into Europeanization, due to their close linkages with high culture (Delanty, 1995) and the various ways in which they are perceived.

However, earlier work on the European Championships and European football does not uncommonly frame the tournament in terms of Europeanization processes (see Horne, 2010) and as a site for both *horizontal* and *vertical* 'top-down' (i.e., promoting good relations between nations, or the spread of standardized best practice templates for host nations) and 'bottom-up' (a European consciousness or awareness) processes (Manzenreiter and Spitaler, 2010). Concerning the latter, Mittag and Legrand (2010) question whether the Euros may have contributed towards the Europeanization of football and reach the argument that football has the *potential* to create a level of European consciousness. Though, whilst football undoubtedly has an important role to play in modern Europe, what is most central in this book's context is 'Europeanization' as an analytical relation that formulates a *backdrop* and ongoing project through which we can understand the European Championships' continual development within and alongside.

What is a sport mega-event and why do the Euros matter?

The second concept we must dedicate space to is 'mega-events'. As Jones and Ponzini (2018: 434) assert, mega-events have, over the last 150 years, been employed as 'instruments to promote and distinguish cities'.

Specifically, they cite the 1851 World Fair's in London and the 1896 Olympic Games in Athens as the earliest examples of this. However, since the mid- and late 1800s, they note that 'mega-events have taken different shapes and forms, evolving over time and with differing focal points'. With mega-events emerging in distinct shapes and forms, this raises the question of what a 'mega-event' in the 2020s essentially is.

In the social study of mega-events, scholars have long discussed what the term means and how it should be defined (Hall, 1989; Müller, 2015; Roche, 2000; Horne, 2007). In order to better understand, throughout this book, *how* and *why* the European Championships reinforces – as we argue – a number of mega-event related trends, we seek to provide a brief account here summarizing these debates. Importantly, this is not motivated by an ambition to 'settle' these debates. Instead, this is to provide an overview of the definitional components, attributes or indicators that are deployed in the pre-existing scholarship. Further, this concurrently demonstrates the *breadth* and *width* of mega-events within and across contemporary social, urban and political realms and mediascapes, which we try to capture in this book.

As we shall return to, we consistently adhere to Roche's (2000: 1, emphasis added) classic definition of 'mega-events' as: 'large-scale, cultural (including commercial and sporting) events, which have a *dramatic character, mass popular appeal* and *international significance*'. Yet there are some other important aspects of mega-events that are left out from this definition. For example, Gold and Gold (2011: 1) understand mega-events as cultural and sporting festivals that 'affect whole economies', whereas Hall's (1989) definition remains more focused on tourism and host city branding. Hall also distinguishes between special, hallmark and mega-events.

Müller (2015) interrogated the meaning of mega-events when he systematically reviewed and synthesized a series of definitions available in the literature. He proposed that mega-events are: 'ambulatory occasions of a fixed duration that attract a large number of visitors, have a large mediated reach, come with large costs and have large impacts on the built environment and the population' (p. 638). Here, an event's 'fixed duration' is a key dimension, because it speaks to the *temporality* of mega-events, which is typically restricted to a specific amount of time (e.g., one year for European Capital of Culture or one month for the Olympics). This, however, does not mean that there are not important pre- and post-event social dimensions of mega-events that live on, beyond the event's actual duration.

Moreover, Müller (2015) also suggests that it is possible to distinguish between *major*, *mega* and *giga*-events. Interestingly, it is here that he notes that the Olympics is the only 'giga-event', whereas he observes how the European Championships and the World Cup can be considered to be increasingly similar in terms of size when classified according to his matrix of visitor attractiveness, mediated reach, cost and transformation (p. 636).

In sum, we contend that mega-events mean different things to different people. However, what this discussion illustrates accurately is the inherently *multidimensional* nature of mega-events. Regardless of which attributes one emphasizes, the available definitions tell us something about how mega-events cut right across urban spaces and life (built environment and transformations), economies and tourism (cf. Hall, 1989) and the global media landscapes ('mediated reach'). They demonstrate how mega-events are typically time-specific, extraordinary or exceptional events that are global or continental occasions. And, indeed, as Jones and Ponzini (2018: 435) allude to: 'intriguingly, the importance of the actual content of the event itself has come to be nearly replaced by the broader desired/perceived outputs and effects of the event'. This is especially true about *sport* mega-events which now encompass much more than 'just' *sport*.

In making a return to Roche's (2000) definition, which is followed throughout this book, the attributes he includes are *dramatic character*, *mass popular appeal* and *international significance*. One question that surfaces relates to how this can be applied to the present-day European Championships. Whilst this (naturally) will become increasingly clear throughout this book, it can be argued that first, in terms of its *dramatic character*, that the European Championships rests much upon its ability to create defining and dramatic moments of football in front of mass crowds (see O'Brien, 2021). On a basic level, the event marks a moment in which the best national teams and athletes in Europe compete against each other (Kennedy, 2017). Moreover, the dramatic character of the Euros is much related to the wider political economy of football, since drama is desired, marketed and a key part of the 'football product' (ibid.). For Euro 2008, 'Expect Emotions' was selected as the tournament's official motto (Lauss and Szigetvari, 2010), and the Championship's opening ceremonies typically compose spectacular occasions in which narratives of the host country (or countries) are showcased in a dramaturgical manner.

Second, concerning *mass popular appeal*, the European Championships appeal to a variety of publics who consume the event in different ways, whether this is through stadium attendance or through 'traditional' or 'new' media (Chapters 3 and 4). This is aided by UEFA's array of broadcasting partners globally and was illustrated by Euro 2020, which was broadcast in 229 territories and reached a cumulative live match audience of 5.2 billion (UEFA, 2021). Additionally, the event and its distinctive spaces are specifically designed and choreographed to be entertaining, packed with fun and loaded with consumption opportunities in order to appeal to mass publics (Lauss and Szigetvari, 2010), including VIPs, tourists, local residents and even fans of teams that did *not* necessarily qualify for the tournament (Millward, 2010).

Third, the Euros are *internationally significant* for a host of reasons. For example, the event is associated with both material and representational legacies and legacy discourses that outlive the month-long tournament itself. The tournament's broadcasting and sponsorships rights, as touched upon, are embedded in the global marketplace where it attracts widespread interest (Horne, 2010). The tournament has also been a site for protest (Lee Ludvigsen, 2022a), and in certain cases, its hosting rights have been pursued (and secured) by states who have sought to enhance their position in the international system and use the event as a vehicle for diplomatic purposes or soft power (Rookwood, 2022). Meanwhile, the efforts to ensure the tournament is secure and safe comprise some of the most complex security operations globally (Lee Ludvigsen, 2022a; Klauser, 2017).

To be clear, we apply Roche's (2000) definition to the European Championships here not because there is any serious doubt within academic circles about whether the event should or should not be considered a '*mega-event*'. Rather, this has been done for the purpose of showcasing how this tournament – *despite* its regular position in the shadows of the Olympics and the World Cup – is of an enormous scale and breadth and matters not merely as a key component of European football or popular culture, but as a commodified 'media event' (ibid.: 5) with associated political and socio-urban projects in modern societies. As we proceed, this is exactly what we seek to capture across this text, and this book will cover key trends speaking to mediation, digitalization, international relations and security, to name a few.

Ultimately, this discussion also reminds us of why mega-events remain so popular in (late-) modernity and are sociologically important. They cut right across the 'popular cultures of cities, sport, tourism and the media' (Roche, 2000: 1) which, essentially, must be considered central topics of the mainstream, contemporary social sciences. In this respect, this book seeks to interrogate an array of mainstream topics through a critical analysis of an event which is 'one of the world's most important sporting events – even beyond the borders of Europe' (Mittag and Legrand, 2010: 709).

Research approach and contributions

We begin this section with some notes on this book's approach. This necessitates a reiteration of what exactly this book is – or tries to do. Essentially, this exploratory research examines social and political issues or trends in the context of sport mega-events. Hence, it is possible to understand this monograph as a case study – where the European Championships feature as the case – which contains multiple 'mini-case studies' across its respective chapters (e.g., cases or examples of specific tournaments). Case study research opens up for the flexible use of various data sources (Yin, 2012) and, upon proceeding, we draw from rich and robust yet diverse material. This includes documentary data (i.e., bid books, official reports) published on key stakeholders' official channels and web-sources. Occasionally, we also draw upon interview quotes provided in journalistic accounts, essentially allowing for what Heaton (2008) calls qualitative secondary data analysis (see Lee Ludvigsen, 2022b).

Notwithstanding, mega-event and case study research also allow for methodological innovation and synthesization. Thus, in line with this book's appreciation of 'the digital', in Chapters 3 and 4, we approach our methodological choices through a digital sociological turn (Lupton, 2014; Marres, 2017) by employing approaches that reflect digital technological developments, as well as the Euros footprint on social media which, for Euro 2020, involved over 279 million impressions on UEFA's social media and 800,000 clicks through UEFA's website (UEFA, n.d.). More specifically, and whilst simultaneously reflecting Millward's (2017) call for sociologists to find the most appropriate ways of capturing social media data, we draw upon automatically collected data through Twitter Academic Application Programming Interface (API) (Twitter, 2022) in R (for academicTwitteR see Barrie and Ho, 2022; RStudio Team, 2022) and trough YouTube API (YouTube, 2022) in YouTube Data Tools (Rieder, 2015). Some of the visualizations in these chapters were generated by using R, whilst others were created on Tableau (2022). This digital sociological approach also informs parts of Chapter 6, where we automatically collected tweets on R and subsequently explored them by using RapidMiner (Mierswa and Klinkenberg, 2022) and VADER (Hutto and Gilbert, 2014) to automatically classify their sentiment during the days surrounding UEFA's postponement announcement of Euro 2020 due to the Covid-19 pandemic (17 March 2020).

Finally, as case study research remains compatible with traditional 'desk-based' research approaches, we also utilize a wider set of literatures that reflects the inter- (or even post-) disciplinary interest in sport mega-events, drawing from diverse literatures in the fields of the sociology of sport, event management, political science, media and communication studies and sport management.

As expanded on in the book's conclusion (Chapter 7), this book primarily extends three fields of study. First, this book contributes an analysis of how forms of popular culture can seriously supplement the study of European culture, politics and cooperation and alter consumption and broadcasting practices in sport. Second, by uniquely bridging the key premises from digital sociology and political sociology, the book makes an original addition to the wider sport mega-event scholarship. This is one of the first academic books focusing exclusively on the European Championships and the *multiple* social issues that emerge (or have emerged) in this event's context. As hinted upon, we know comparatively much about the Olympic Games and the World Cup and their sociologies and political histories (Boykoff, 2016; Goldblatt, 2016; Chadwick et al., 2022). In a way, this book's advanced sociology of the European Championships is not only an original account of this particular mega-event, but it represents a productive resource for future work to be conducted on the Euros and sport mega-events. Third, this research advances the extant literature focused on European football. In particular, it empirically documents again *why* European football is a sociologically valuable domain for the interpretation of wider trends 'beyond' football (Millward, 2009; King, 2003; Levermore and Millward, 2007).

A roadmap for this book

The book is divided into seven chapters. As stated, it is primarily concerned with social issues and changes that have emerged within or around the context of the European Championships in men's football over the last two decades. Therefore, each chapter addresses either one or more inter-related topics. Yet, as reflective of the dynamic world of sport, there are *many* social trends and issues that warrant serious exploration and addressing them all is – perhaps unsurprisingly – beyond this book's scope. Nevertheless, this informs the research agenda that we subsequently intend to launch here.

Due to our study's scope, we focus primarily on the men's Euros. First, this is explained by reasons of brevity and this book's short and sharp nature. Second, we remain adamant that a sociology of the Euros remains a *continual project*. Therefore, with the women's Euros composing an important site for sociological and historical research (Bell, 2019; de Oliviera et al., 2022), it is undeniable that the women's tournament is worthy of a book in itself, as the Euros juggernaut continues throughout the 2020s and 2030s. Moreover, other events organized by UEFA like youth and amateur categories, futsal, eSports, UEFA Champions League (UCL) and club competitions also deserve further attention, but do not compose a key focus of this book.

Then, the main themes we address include the changing nature of broadcasting, digital media and consumption (see Petersen-Wagner, 2022) cohosting and joint bids (see Byun et al., 2019), environmental policies (see Orr and Ross, 2022) and emergency politics. Collectively, these represent social changes that we have chosen to explore further on the basis that they have recently been identified by scholars in other event-specific contexts (predominantly the Olympics and the World Cup) (e.g., Tang and Cooper, 2018; Chadwick et al., 2022) and because they remain compatible with wider calls and research agendas in the field (Wise and Maguire,

2022; Ludvigsen et al., 2022), though they are concurrently yet to be fully explored – if at all – in the context of the European Championships. As Roche (2017: 55) submits, social changes influence the 'nature and production' of mega-events, however, 'social changes "does not sleep"', underscoring the need for a consistent inquiry into mega-events' social changes.

More generally, as hinted upon, the selected themes are also compatible with the research agendas located in the wider social scientific fields of digital sociology (Lupton, 2014; Marres, 2017) and political sociology (Gilchrist et al., 2015). Here, the former concerns itself, broadly, with the impact of the 'digital' on individual and social life, whereas the latter concerns itself with the nexus between societies, social relations and the institutional dimensions of politics (Barrie, 2021). Both for the digital and political sociologies, mega-events should be considered as highly illuminating sites of inquiry, and the cross-pollination of the underlying principles from digital sociology and political sociology thus informs this book's exploration of the digital (Chapters 3, 4) and political manifestations (Chapters 2, 5, 6) of the Euros which, again, direct and (re-)organize the social realities, changes and impacts of the Euros.

Whereas we have signposted towards some of the extant work conducted on the European Championships already, Chapter 2 reviews this literature more thematically, whilst also positioning the Euros and its expansion in a socio-political and historical frame spanning the 1950s to the present day. The chapter also unpacks the key process of commercialization which characterizes modern elite sport before it explores concepts of power, authority and governance between key actors in the Euros.

Drawing from social media analyses, Chapters 3 and 4 examine the nexus between the Euros, consumption, media and digital platforms. Here, Chapter 3 explores how 'traditional' media outlets have transcended and acted as complementors on social media platforms like Twitter. This again yields insight into the transformation of broadcasting within new media spaces. Chapter 4 explores another emerging platform, YouTube, and analyses the relevant YouTube playlists in order to provide an insight into how audiences and official broadcasters have transformed their cultural practices in terms of the Euros.

Chapter 5 examines the concept of co-hosting and co-bidding in the context of the Euros. It asks why countries join forces and bid for mega-events and how these alliances are framed. The European Championships has been pioneering when it comes to co-staging events across two (or even 11) countries, as the cases of Netherlands/Belgium (2000), Austria/Switzerland (2008), Ukraine/Poland (2012) and Euro 2020 show. However, this chapter will not only look at the EU and non-EU implications of co-hosting, but the cultural politics of bidding alliances in the case of the Nordic alliances of the 2000s, and it discusses the potential joint UK and Irish bid before Euro 2028.

It is clear that the politics of security and emergency are increasingly embedded in the European Championships. Therefore, Chapter 6 explores how precautionary principles and rhetoric are increasingly articulated in climates of uncertainty at European Championships in relation to three threat categories. The chapter does so by exploring, first, the discourses surrounding Euro 2016 that were staged in France whilst the host country was in a state of emergency following a series of terrorist attacks in Paris in November 2015. Second, the chapter looks at Twitter interactions during the announcement of the postponement of Euro 2020 due to the Covid-19 pandemic. Third, we explore environmental policies and discourses before Germany's Euro 2024 against the backdrop of wider political concerns about climate change and environmental crises.

Chapter 7 presents the book's conclusions and summarizes the key arguments. This concluding chapter also provides an outlook of what the future may hold for the Euros in a turbulent time of change in '(new) Europe' and advances areas of future research. The chapter also reflects on how the book – marrying key ideas from digital sociology and political sociology – contributes to the wider literatures on sport mega-events, football and Europe.

Notes

1 See: www.dailymail.co.uk/sport/football/article-10591685/UEFA-plan-EXPAND-Euros-32-TEAM-tournament-2028.html#:~:text=EXCLUSIVE%3A%20 UEFA%20plan%20to%20EXPAND,talks%20against%20'harming% 20the%20product'&text=UEFA%20are%20to%20expand%20the,following%20 discussions%20with%20member%20nations.
2 Subsequently, UEFA banned Russia from submitting a bid for Euro 2028 and FIFA suspended Russia from international football. See: www.independent.co.uk/ sport/football/russia-uefa-euros-2028-bid-b2069982.html

References

Alpan B, Schwell, A and Sonntag A (eds.) (2015) *The European Football Championship: Mega-Event and Vanity Fair*. Basingstoke: Palgrave.
Arnold R (eds.) (2021) *Russia and the 2018 FIFA World Cup*. London: Routledge.
Bandyopadhyay K, Naha S and Mitra S (eds.) (2018) *FIFA World Cup and Beyond: Sport, Culture, Media and Governance*. Oxon: Routledge.
Barrie C (2021) Political sociology in a time of protest. *Current Sociology* 69(6): 919–942.
Barrie C and Ho JC-T (2022) academictwitteR: An R package to access the Twitter Academic Research Product Track v2 API endpoint. *Journal of Open Source Software* 6(62): 3272.

Beck U and Grande E (2008) *Cosmopolitan Europe*. Cambridge: Polity.

Bell B (2019) Women's Euro 2005 a 'watershed' for women's football in England and a new era for the game? *Sport in History* 39(4): 445–461.

Borneman J and Fowler N (1997) Europeanization. *Annual Review of Anthropology* 26(1): 487–514.

Boykoff J (2014) *Celebration Capitalism and the Olympic Games*. London: Routledge.

Boykoff J (2016) *Power Games: A Political History of the Olympics*. London and New York: Verso Books.

Boykoff J (2020) *Nolympians: Inside the Fight Against Capitalist Mega-Sports in Los Angeles, Tokyo & Beyond*. Nova Scotia: Fernwood Publishing.

Brand A, Niemann A and Spitaler G (2013) The two-track Europeanization of football: EU-level pressures, transnational dynamics and their repercussions within different national contexts. *International Journal of Sport Policy and Politics* 5(1): 95–112.

Brannagan PM and Reiche D (2022) *Qatar and the 2022 FIFA World Cup: Politics, Controversy, Change*. Switzerland: Palgrave Macmillan.

Byun J, Leopkey B and Ellis D (2019) Understanding joint-bids for international large-scale sport events as strategic alliances. *Sport, Business and Management: An International Journal* 10(1): 39–57.

Castells M (1994) European cities, the informational society, and the global economy. *New Left Review* 204: 18–32.

Chadwick S, Widdop P, Anagnostopoulos C and Parnell D (eds.) (2022) *The Business of the FIFA World Cup*. Oxon: Routledge.

Delanty G (1995) *Inventing Europe: Idea, Identity, Reality*. London: Palgrave.

Delanty G (2005) The idea of a cosmopolitan Europe: On the cultural significance of Europeanization. *International Review of Sociology – Revue Internationale de Sociologie* 15(3): 405–421.

de Oliveira JR, de Oliveira Souza MT and Capraro AM (2022) Media coverage and public opinion of hosting a women's football mega-event: The English bid for UEFA Women's Euro 2022. *Sport in Society*: 1–20.

Dunn C (2015) *Football and the Women's World Cup: Organisation, Media and Fandom*. Basingstoke: Palgrave.

Featherstone K (2003) Introduction: In the name of 'Europe'. In: K Featherstone and CM Radaelli (eds.) *The Politics of Europeanization*. Oxford: Oxford University Press, pp. 3–26.

Frawley S and Adair D (eds.) (2013) *Managing the Olympics*. London: Palgrave.

Giddens A (2014) *Turbulent and Mighty Continent: What Future for Europe?* Cambridge: Polity Press.

Gilchrist P, Holden R and Millward P (2015) Special section introduction: The political sociologies of sport. *Sociological Research Online* 20(2): 141–144.

Giulianotti R (1999) *Football: A Sociology of the Global Game*. Cambridge: Polity Press.

Gold JR and Gold MM (2011) *Olympic Cities: City Agendas, Planning, and the World's Games*. London: Routledge.

Goldblatt D (2016) *The Games: A Global History of the Olympics.* London: Pan Macmillan.

Goldblatt D (2019) *The Age of Football.* New York and London: W. W. Norton.

The Guardian (2022) *Boris Johnson Calls for Ukraine to Host Euro 2028 Despite UK-Ireland Bid.* Available at: www.theguardian.com/football/2022/mar/24/boris-johnson-calls-for-ukraine-to-host-euro-2028-despite-uk-ireland-bid-russia.

Hall CM (1989) The definition and analysis of hallmark tourist events. *GeoJournal* 19(3): 263–268.

Hänska M and Bauchowitz S (2019) Can social media facilitate a European public sphere? Transnational communication and the Europeanization of Twitter during the Eurozone crisis. *Social Media+ Society*: 1–14.

Harris J (2018) A Welsh European: Golf, tourism and the remaking of national imaging. *International Journal of Cultural Studies* 21(4): 405–419.

Heaton J (2008) Secondary analysis of qualitative data: An overview. *Historical Social Research/Historische Sozialforschung* 33(3): 33–45.

Horne J (2007) The four 'knowns' of sports mega-events. *Leisure Studies* 26(1): 81–96.

Horne J (2010) Material and representational legacies of sports mega-events: The case of the UEFA EURO™ football championships from 1996 to 2008. *Soccer & Society* 11(6): 854–866.

Horne J and Whannel G (2016) *Understanding the Olympics.* London: Routledge.

Hutto C and Gilbert E (2014) VADER: A parsimonious rule-based model for sentiment analysis of social media text. In: *Eighth International AAAI Conference on Weblogs and Social Media (ICWSM-14). Proceedings of the International AAAI Conference on Web and Social Media*, Vol. 8, No. 1. Ann Arbor, MI: The AAAI Press, pp. 216–225. Available at: https://ojs.aaai.org/index.php/ICWSM/article/view/14550; https://dblp.org/db/conf/icwsm/index.html.

Jones ZM and Ponzini D (2018) Mega-events and the preservation of urban heritage: Literature gaps, potential overlaps, and a call for further research. *Journal of Planning Literature* 33(4): 433–450.

Kassimeris C (2017) Football in Europe: Apolitical UEFA plays politics with football. In: J Hughson, K Moore, R Spaaij and JA Maguire (eds.) *Routledge Handbook of Football Studies.* London: Routledge, pp. 434–444.

Kennedy P (2017) Using Habermas to crack the European football championships. *Sport in Society* 20(3): 355–368.

King A (2003) *The European Ritual: Football in the New Europe.* London: Routledge.

King A (2010) After the crunch: A new era for the beautiful game in Europe? *Soccer & Society* 11(6): 880–891.

Klauser F (2017) *Surveillance and Space.* London: Sage.

Kushnir I (2016) The role of the Bologna Process in defining Europe. *European Educational Research Journal* 15(6): 664–675.

Ladrech R (2002) Europeanization and political parties: Towards a framework for analysis. *Party Politics* 8(4): 389–403.

Lauss G and Szigetvari A (2010) Governing by fun: EURO 2008 and the appealing power of fan zones. *Soccer & Society* 11(6): 737–747.

Lee Ludvigsen, JA (2020) The 'troika of security': Merging retrospective and futuristic 'risk' and 'security' assessments before Euro 2020. *Leisure Studies* 39(6): 844–858.

Lee Ludvigsen JA (2021) Mega-events, expansion and prospects: Perceptions of Euro 2020 and its 12-country hosting format. *Journal of Consumer Culture*: 1–19.

Lee Ludvigsen JA (2022a) *Sport Mega-Events, Security and Covid-19: Securing the Football World*. Oxon: Routledge.

Lee Ludvigsen JA (2022b) When 'the show' cannot go on: An investigation into sports mega-events and responses during the pandemic crisis. *International Review for the Sociology of Sport* 57(4): 497–514.

Lee Ludvigsen JA, Rookwood J and Parnell D (2022) The sport mega-events of the 2020s: Governance, impacts and controversies. *Sport in Society* 25(4): 705–711.

Levermore R and Millward P (2007) Official policies and informal transversal networks: Creating 'pan-European identifications' through sport? *The Sociological Review* 55(1): 144–164.

Lupton D (2014) *Digital Sociology*. London: Routledge.

Manzenreiter W and Spitaler G (2010) Governance, citizenship and the new European Football championships: The European spectacle. *Soccer & Society* 11(6): 695–708.

Marres N (2017) *Digital Sociology: The Reinvention of Social Research*. Cambridge: Polity.

McNeill D (2014) *New Europe: Imagined Spaces*. London: Routledge.

Mierswa I and Klinkenberg R (2022) *RapidMiner Studio* [Educational License]. 9.10 ed. Available at: https://rapidminer.com.

Millward P (2009) *Getting into Europe: Identification, Prejudice and Politics in English Football Culture*. Staarbrucken: VDM Verlag.

Millward P (2010) The limits to cosmopolitanism': English football fans at Euro 2008. In: D Burdsey (ed.) *Race, Ethnicity and Football: Persisting Debates and Emergent Issues*. London: Routledge, pp. 163–174.

Millward P (2017) Football and social media: Fanzines, fan scenes and supporter protest movements in elite English football. In: J Hughson, K Moore, R Spaaij and J Maguire (eds.) *Routledge Handbook of Football Studies*. Abingdon: Routledge, pp. 189–199.

Mittag J and Legrand B (2010) Towards a Europeanization of football? Historical phases in the evolution of the UEFA European Football Championship. *Soccer & Society* 11(6): 709–722.

Müller M (2015) What makes an event a mega-event? Definitions and sizes. *Leisure Studies* 34(6): 627–642.

O'Brien J (2021) *Euro Summits: The Story of the UEFA European Championships 1960 to 2021*. Sussex: Pitch Publishing.

Orr M and Ross WJ (2022) Assessing climate suitability of three cities for the 2027 women's World Cup. *Case Studies in Sport Management* 11(1): S14–S18.

Petersen-Wagner R (2022) The business of FIFA World Cup: Digital and social media. In: S Chadwick, D Parnell, P Widdop, et al. (eds.) *Routledge Handbook of Business of FIFA World Cup*. London: Routledge.

Rieder B (2015) *YouTube Data Tools*. 1.22 ed. Available at: https://tools.digitalmethods.net/netvizz/youtube/index.php.

Roche M (2000) *Mega-Events and Modernity: Olympics and Expos in the Growth of Global Culture*. London: Routledge.

Roche M (2017) *Mega-Events and Social Change: Spectacle, Legacy and Public Culture*. Manchester: Manchester University Press.

Rookwood J (2022) From sport-for-development to sports mega-events: Conflict, authoritarian modernisation and statecraft in Azerbaijan. *Sport in Society* 25(4): 847–866.

RStudio Team (2022) *RStudio: Integrated Development for R*. 2022.7.1.554 ed. Boston.

Sassatelli M (2008) European cultural space in the European cities of culture: Europeanization and cultural policy. *European Societies* 10(2): 225–245.

Tableau (2022) *Tableau Desktop*. 2022.1 ed. Available at: https://www.tableau.com.

Tang T and Cooper R (2018) The most social games: Predictors of social media uses during the 2016 Rio Olympics. *Communication & Sport* 6(3): 308–330.

Twitter (2022) *Academic Research Access*. Available at: https://developer.twitter.com/en/products/twitter-api/academic-research (accessed 13/05/2022).

UEFA (2019) *What UEFA Does*. Available at: www.uefa.com/insideuefa/about-uefa/what-uefa-does/.

UEFA (2021) *UEFA EURO 2020 Impresses with 5.2 billion Cumulative Global Live Audience*. Available at: https://www.uefa.com/insideuefa/about-uefa/news/026d-132519672495-56a014558e80-1000--uefa-euro-2020-impresses-with-5-2-billion-cumulative-global-liv/.

UEFA (2022) *Israel Football Association*. Available at: www.uefa.com/insideuefa/national-associations/isr/ (accessed 31/05/2022).

UEFA (n.d.) *UEFA Euro 2020 Went Viral: A Special Tournament: On the Pitch, and on Social Media*. Available at: https://editorial.uefa.com/resources/0276-15769ffa5879-a62705924d6d-1000/220225_uefa_euro_2020_goes_viral_20220624112434.pdf?fbclid=IwAR1L3-V2MCoBG5NCN2MDc6znwadasX1WY6lYwwyJa3_CxA667d97zodPVt8.

Wise N and Maguire K (eds.) (2022) *A Research Agenda for Event Impacts*. Cheltenham: Edward Elgar Publishing.

Włoch R (2013) UEFA as a new agent of global governance: A case study of relations between UEFA and the Polish Government against the background of the UEFA EURO 2012. *Journal of Sport and Social Issues* 37(3): 297–311.

Yair G (2019) Douze point: Eurovisions and Euro-divisions in the Eurovision song contest – review of two decades of research. *European Journal of Cultural Studies* 22(5–6): 1013–1029.

Yin RK (2012) *Applications of Case Study Research* [3rd edition]. Los Angeles: Sage.

YouTube (2022) *Data API*. Available at: https://developers.google.com/youtube/v3 (accessed 12/04/2022).

2 The rise of the Euros in a political, sociological and historical context

Introduction

Since the 1980s, sport mega-events have undergone political economic transformations, most notably in relation to the restructuring of their media and commercial partnerships and the profitable aspirations of sport's governing bodies (Doidge et al., 2019). As this chapter maintains, the modern European Championships has not been exempted from these transformations. Yet, this mega-event – which first emerged in Europe's post-war milieu – has not always been a hyper-commercialized occasion that can be considered to be in direct competition with the FIFA World Cup (Mittag and Legrand, 2010). In Chapter 1, we underlined the sociological importance of the Euros whilst we located the event as co-existent with pre-existing conceptualizations or ideas of what 'Europe' is or means, and within the universe of sport mega-events. Still, it remains imperative to provide a *tour d'horizon* of the Euros' origins and rise, its position within academic research, and the event's political economy in elite sport's neoliberal context (see Giulianotti, 2005).

To do this, this chapter unpacks the Euros' journey from its 'humble beginnings' (cf. Mittag and Legrand, 2010) into a commercialized, mediatized, symbolic and deeply politicized mega-event. Specifically, it borrows ideas from the important work of Włoch (2013), who conceptualizes UEFA as a 'global governor' which has the power to shape the interests of nation-states and corporations alike in the international system. Finally, it concludes by arguing for a coherent and contemporary sociology of the European Championships in the twenty-first century.

A story of expansion

This section summarizes the emergence and enlargement of the European Championships. Whilst other authors provide far longer and more detailed

DOI: 10.4324/9781003359098-2

accounts on the tournament's historical origins and predecessors (see O'Brien, 2021; Mittag and Legrand, 2010; Vonnard, 2014), it is possible, for reasons of brevity, to delineate the rise of the European Championships according to four distinctive phases (see Mittag and Legrand, 2010).

First, there are the tournament's 'humble beginnings' between 1955 and 1968. Second, the period of the event's growing attraction and consolidation between 1968–1980, fuelled by increased media attention and profitable aspirations. Third, a period of new approaches and further expansion between 1980 and 1996 characterized by a changing live sport/media landscape (see also Chapter 3). Finally, there is the post-1996 period in which the European Championships emerged as a direct competitor to the FIFA World Cup (ibid.: 713–718).

Tracing the origins of the European Championships back to the post-war period means that one must view them in the context of a Europe characterized by a war-torn environment, a growing divide between East and West Cold War politics (Kennedy, 2017) and the emergence of global governance institutions in deliberate attempts to boost (inter-)national economies (Weiss, 2000). However, at the same time in the football world, European football had also started to become increasingly professionalized whilst structurally, the foundation of UEFA in 1954 – as the governing body of European football – 'provided new conditions and possibilities for setting up a continental competition' (Vonnard, 2014: 599; see also Vonnard, 2020).

One of UEFA's aims, which became another solidified factor within the football world, related to the development of unity and solidarities in European football during the Cold War divisions that characterized Europe (Kassimeris, 2017). As Vonnard (2020: 1) writes, UEFA was not merely set up to administer the European game, but to impact 'more generally the European integration process'. For contextual purposes, at this time in the wider football world, since 1916 the South American associations had organized themselves through the South American Football Confederation (CONMEBOL) (Petersen-Wagner et al., 2018) in response to European nations' dominance in FIFA. Meanwhile, FIFA itself saw UEFA's foundation as the potential emergence of a rival organization (Olsson, 2011).

Notwithstanding these, early ideas and initiatives related to what is now known as the European Championships existed even before the Second World War's end. Most notably, they were advocated by the French football administrator and UEFA General Secretary, Henri Delaunay, who pioneered the efforts to start up a competition for European national teams. Yet, although the idea of a European Championships perpetuated throughout the early 1950s, it failed to immediately materialize, even after the formal foundation of UEFA, partly due to the lack of support from the individual football associations (Mittag and Legrand, 2010).

Then, after Henri Delaunay's death in 1955, his son Pierre Delaunay continued to pursue the vision of a European Nations' Cup as he took over his father's post as UEFA General Secretary (O'Brien, 2021). For Pierre and the other champions of the new competition for national teams, its materialization was considered important not only for the purposes of further advancing UEFA's structure, but also in order to forge better relations between European football associations (Vonnard and Quin, 2017). Thus, Pierre proposed his father's idea at the UEFA Congress in Lisbon in July 1956, though with limited success due to concerns that a new European tournament would congest and disrupt the football calendar and the teams' World Cup preparations. However, by 1957, the proponents of a European Championships had won a majority of 15 votes to 13, and so: 'the realization of the first Nations' Cup came to pass, and in honour of its intellectual father it was proposed to be named the "Henri Delaunay Cup"' (Mittag and Legrand, 2010: 713).

Since the inaugural 1960 European Nations' Cup took place as a four-team, four-day knock-out competition between 6 and 10 July – with fixtures held in Paris and Marseille – the tournament has consistently continued to expand both organizationally and commercially (Lee Ludvigsen, 2021a). By the 1980 edition, the number of qualified teams increased from four to eight, then from eight to 16 before Euro 1996 and to 24 before Euro 2016. In the years after 1960, the tournament also migrated between Spain (1964), Italy (1968), Belgium (1972), Yugoslavia (1976) and Italy (1980) before it made a return to France in 1984 (Table 2.1). Importantly, by 1968, the tournament's name had also officially changed from the 'European Nations' Cup' to the '*European Championships*'. Further, as Law (2014) writes, from 1984 the increased mobilities of fans at the Euros – whilst fuelling 'hooliganism' concerns – also meant that UEFA now more distinctively started to aligned itself to EU's ideal of 'unity in diversity' (p. 205).

As we discuss later, the economic aspects of the tournament were also enlarged, as the prize money, broadcasting rights and revenue figures consistently increased (Mittag and Legrand, 2010). In a similar fashion, the women's European Championships have since 1984 had a changing history, with the first official event played with home and away matches with a size four ball, and having only 35-minute halves (UEFA, 2013). In the following tournament (1987 in Norway), the halves were increased by five minutes and games were played with a size 5 ball, but it was not until 1991 that games changed to 45-minute halves and the tournament was given full European Championships status, officially changing its name to UEFA Women's Championship (ibid.). As shall be discussed next, in accordance with this football mega-event's prominence in the world of sport, it has also attracted academic interest.

Table 2.1 A summary of Men's and Women's European Championships, 1960–2025

Year	Gender	Host country	Competing teams
1960	Men's	France	4
1964	Men's	Spain	4
1968	Men's	Italy	4
1972	Men's	Belgium	4
1976	Men's	Yugoslavia	4
1980	Men's	Italy	8
1984	Men's	France	8
	Women's	Sweden/England/ Denmark/Italy	4
1987	Women's	Norway	4
1988	Men's	West Germany	8
1989	Women's	West Germany	8
1991	Women's	Denmark	8
1992	Men's	Sweden	8
1993	Women's	Italy	8
1995	Women's	England/Germany/ Norway/Sweden	4
1996	Men's	England	16
1997	Women's	Norway/Sweden	8
2000	Men's	Netherlands/Belgium	16
2001	Women's	Germany	8
2004	Men's	Portugal	16
2005	Women's	England	8
2008	Men's	Austria/Switzerland	16
2009	Women's	Finland	12
2012	Men's	Poland/Ukraine	16
2013	Women's	Sweden	12
2016	Men's	France	24
2017	Women's	Netherlands	16
2020 (staged in 2021 due to Covid-19)	Men's	11 European countries	24
2021 (staged in 2022 due to Covid-19)	Women's	England	16
2024	Men's	Germany	24
2025	Women's	To be decided in December 2022	16

Source: UEFA (2022a, 2022b)

Existing and emerging research on the Euros

In Chapter 1, it was argued that the European Championships – when juxta-posed with the World Cup and the Olympics – has been left largely under-researched. This does not mean, however, that there is an absence of social research on this mega-event. As this section demonstrates, social scientists have since the 1990s increasingly responded to some of the social issues that have emerged in relation to the tournament (Millward, 2010). The earlier discussion underscores that the origins of the Euros have been covered. Yet most of the existing research focuses on the European Championships in what Mittag and Legrand label the 'fourth phase' (1996–to date).

In context of the nexus between the media, media coverage and identity politics, Poulton (2004) uses the Euros as an entry to explore expressions of national identity in British television coverage of the Euro 1996. Interestingly, Poulton's findings suggest that mega-events like the Euros can be considered 'mediated patriot games', where nations are pitted up against each other with matches being framed in terms of 'us versus them'. Similarly, Maguire and Poulton's (1999) analysis of English newspapers suggests that the press coverage during the same event appeared more divisive than uniting and could serve to reinforce (in England) an anti-European sentiment. Meanwhile, Rek-Woźniak and Woźniak's (2020) analysis of the *BBC*'s documentary 'Stadiums of Hate' before Euro 2012 also demonstrates the power of the media in creating dominant discourses or moral panics before or during the Euros. The media thus has the potential to socially construct ideas of spectacle (Marivoet, 2006), imagined communities and fear (see Chapters 3 and 6).

In the Euros' 'fourth phase', and particularly in the post-2001 'war on terror' era, scholars also increasingly started to examine the security and surveillance practices at European Championships. Since 2001, security complexes at sport mega-events have generally intensified. This enhanced the need to 'secure' events and crowds from 'terrorism' and 'hooliganism' (Millward et al., 2022). Against this canvas, Klauser (2011) examines how best practices of security and surveillance were transferred from the 2006 World Cup in Germany and Euro 2008 in Switzerland/Austria. Thereby he provides insight into how practices of knowledge transfer occur in between European mega-events and stakeholders. Meanwhile, Lauss and Szigetvari (2010) and Hagemann (2010) examine the intersections between security and emergency policies at Euro 2008 and how these policies simultaneously served purposes of branding and commercial activities. Supporting these findings, Lee Ludvigsen (2020, 2021b, 2022) also investigates the concept of security at Euro 2020, which was postponed due to the Covid-19 pandemic. He argues that this event relied upon increasingly standardized policy templates and reinforced the European Championships' position as 'testing grounds' for new security methods, relationships and policies (Lee Ludvigsen, 2022). Other aspects of the Euros that have been examined, meanwhile, are its fluid conceptions of legacies (Horne, 2010; Kossakowski, 2019).

Finally, in the ethnographic tradition, Millward (2010) researched English fans who had travelled to Euro 2008 (a tournament England failed to qualify for) in order to understand the notions and limits of 'cosmopolitanism' among this fan group. Meanwhile, Giulianotti's (1995) account of Scottish fans travelling to the 1992 Euros in Sweden provides an insight into the contested and complex nature of supporter cultures and particularly that of carnivalesque behaviour which possesses different meanings according to fans, the media and policing actors.

Thus, much in accordance with the wider scholarship on mega-events, social research on the Euros can predominantly be traced back to the early 1990s. Visibly, within this literature, an array of mainstream sociological issues has been explored through the use of existing theoretical oeuvres (for example Elias, Anderson, Habermas, Cohen): identity, nationalism, security, fan culture, cosmopolitanism and social control. Yet these topics have predominantly been examined separately. Meanwhile, some emerging topics within the wider (digital) football studies or sport mega-event scholarship, including 'digitized' football consumption (Lawrence and Crawford, 2018), co-hosting (Wise and Lee Ludvigsen, 2022) and environmental politics have been assigned less research.

Overall, whilst our reading of the literature reaffirms the European Championships' sociological worth it is simultaneously striking that a *coherent, critical* and *contemporary* sociology of the Euros has hitherto been underdeveloped. Crucially, this ties back into the book's aims accounted for in Chapter 1, but in order to proceed with this, one key process within the world of sport has to be unpacked. That is commercialization.

Commercialization and magnified corporate interest

Following Kennedy (2017), the Euros should be situated in the material context of late capitalist society, particularly due to UEFA's networked evolution that is directed towards the reproduction of capital. In other words, it is impossible to develop a sophisticated sociological understanding of the contemporary European Championships without critically accounting for the tournament's position within the environment of sport and football's wider political economy. This is especially so in a time where UEFA – who owns the event's commercial rights – has been described as a 'hybrid international organization that combines elements of nongovernmental activities with those more typical of transnational corporations' (Włoch, 2013: 298).

In parallel with processes of globalization, sport has developed as a commercialized leisure and entertainment industry that is tightly interconnected to corporate media and commodity corporate finances (Rahman and Lockwood, 2011). Alongside this, '[t]he contemporary structures of football are geared toward global consumption' (Giulianotti, 2002: 42). This has implications for (football) mega-events. Therefore, much like other large-scale sporting events and sport governing bodies, the European Championships and UEFA are characterized by their commercial activities and links to sponsors, commercial broadcasting networks and media platforms.

In this respect, other academics have outlined mega-events as archetypical projects of 'celebration capitalism' (Boykoff, 2014, 2016) or 'festival capitalism', which is characterized by the use of euphoric sporting festivals for the advancements of public/private partnerships and free-market interests (Giulianotti et al., 2015). This has consequently tied sport, and particularly football, to the overarching global consumer culture. As Giulianotti and Numerato (2018: 230) write:

> Powerful corporate interests drive the founding and global spread of glamorous sport events and tournaments – from the Olympic Games and football's World Cup finals through to numerous 'national' leagues. . . . Yet, these commercial processes are not uncontested but instead germinate unease, criticism and protest over the influence of capital on how sport is experienced, played and organized.

As such, it is possible to draw tangible parallels between the commercialization of the Euros, Olympics (Boykoff, 2016) and the World Cup (Cornelissen, 2007), especially with regards to how the IOC and FIFA gradually embraced the principles of global neoliberalism since the 1970s and 1980s (Eick, 2011; Boykoff, 2016). Similarly, the social history of the European Championships demonstrates how UEFA increasingly has opened up for and consciously pursued commercial activities (Horne, 2010).

Whilst televised broadcasting of live football matches had begun to generate financial profits already in the 1980s (Włoch, 2013), it could be argued that the commercialization of the Euros experienced a take-off period and mushroomed throughout the 1990s. Naturally, this was much assisted by (and dependent on) the interest from media platforms and transnational corporations, and it quickly led to a growth in revenue from the European Championships' commercial rights, broadcasting and hospitality. Indeed, since the 1990s, some of the tournament's official sponsors have included transnational companies such as McDonald's, Coca-Cola, Carlsberg, MasterCard and Hyundai (Horne, 2010), exemplifying how global enterprises have sought to utilize the growing worldwide exposure of an (ever-)expanding sport mega-event, which certainly reaffirms the commercial, symbolic and financial value of the 'Euros-product'.

The figures provided by Kennedy (2017: 356) show that, over the course of the six tournaments between 1992 and 2012, there was a 34-fold increase in revenue for UEFA, as the total revenue from the Euros ballooned from €41 million (1992) to €1389.2 million in 2012. More recent figures suggest that these numbers have increased apace, with Euro 2016 and Euro 2020 generating €1916 million and €1882.5 million respectively (Statista, 2022). With the potential visibility provided by a European Championships broadcasted in 229 territories, it could also be observed that, for the Euros' 2020 edition – which included six global partners, six national sponsors and five licensees (Statista, 2021) – global mobile app-based companies such as Tik-Tok and Just Eat were among the sponsors (Chadwick and Widdop, 2021), possibly suggesting a new trend within mega-event sponsorship in the digital era (see Chapter 3 and 4).

However, the commercialism embedded in the European Championships also has a range of socio-spatial impacts on host cities. For instance, Hageman (2010) points out that event spheres such as stadiums and fan zones are increasingly dressed up in a 'commercial display' where sponsors are embedded in a 'temporary brand world' packed with consumption opportunities for fans, including merchandise and products from official licensees. Essentially, these branded spheres are highly protected and facilitated for through specific policies and imposed requirements. Typically, these are conditions that must be guaranteed by the countries who are awarded the tournament's hosting rights by UEFA, which reinforces the facilitation of spaces free from the presence of rivalling brands/products to those of UEFA's partners (ibid.).

As such, the commercialism of the Euros, which has strengthened its brand and status, touches the surface of another issue this chapter turns to next. That is the relationship between the key actors of the European spectacle and the political structures in which the tournaments are embedded that have an array of (in)tangible social implications.

Power play: mapping the key actors in the field

Each edition of the European Championships (re)activates a myriad of interactions and connections between diverse key actors that set the standards for, or assist, the bidding or organization of the event (Chapter 5). For example, as UEFA's requirements book for Euro 2024 bidders states, the staging of the tournament not only depends on a 'complex preparation' but cooperation between private and public actors across international, national and local levels (UEFA, 2017, Sector 5: 1). Thus, as Law (2014: 204) writes, '[t]he football field is never an autonomous zone, set free from other fields of power. International football is always a field of tensions'. From a political sociological perspective, this flurry of actors remains especially illuminating as all this opens up questions speaking broadly to how political and sub-political actors claim authority and exert their power *upon* societies and populations (Gilchrist et al., 2015; Chatzigianni, 2018).

In a way, it can even be argued that the Euros serve as an extremely pertinent window for understanding how nation-states (representing host nations
or bidders) and non-state actors (e.g., sport governing bodies administrating
the event) – which we focus on here – and transnational corporations (TNCs)
interact in an era of global governance (Włoch, 2013, 2020; Lee Ludvigsen,
2022; Giulianotti and Robertson, 2012) and impact societal elements in the
form of host communities, local residents, fans and consumers. Furthermore,
as alluded to, other powerful actors with distinctive interest and levels of
power may also be situated within the organization of the European Championships where they exercise their authority (Chatzigianni, 2018). This
includes FIFA – as the international governing body of football – but also
broadcasters (see Chapters 3 and 4) and sponsors (Pearson, 2012) in addition
to public security agencies (Klauser, 2011; Tsoukala, 2009) and European
organizations like the Council of Europe (Lee Ludvigsen, 2022; UEFA, n.d.).
Collectively, these actors, and their relations, shape and dictate the Euros'
organization, outcomes and resources.

A key starting point for understanding the relations between nation-states
and non-state actors remains the aforementioned commercialization of
mega-events which co-exists with the evolving international political significance of events. First, as mentioned, UEFA (but also FIFA and IOC) as
the key governing bodies of sport have, since the 1980s, started to work
closer with transnational corporations in the pursuit of profit. This development must be viewed in context of sport governing bodies' *ownership* of the
events' mediatized product. Yet sport's governing bodies have also assured
nation-states that hosting events can be desirable for countries' legacies and
economic impacts (Włoch, 2020).

Second, it is important to consider the position, perspectives and policies
of nation-states. Since the 1990s, some countries have utilized mega-events
in order to showcase their 'growing (geo)political and economic potential'
(ibid.: 46) to global audiences. Hence, whereas mega-events long have been
staged to promote national power elites' visions of progress in modernity
(Roche, 2000), for some states, mega-events have been employed by nation-
states who strategically have considered events as tools that can assist the
'politics of attraction' and thereby enhance states' position in global affairs
(Grix and Lee, 2013; Chapter 5).

Following Włoch (2013, 2020), these trends, as applied to the European
Championships, have enabled a context in which UEFA has increased its
power on the global stage. Here, UEFA's *power* derives much from their
ownership of the media and commercial and intellectual property rights of
the tournaments. Thus, states pursuing power must conform to the event
owner's conditions. Despite this, inter-dependencies emerge: UEFA still
depends on states and their territories for the event to be successfully

coordinated and staged. However, through the competitive application and bidding processes where states must provide guarantees that they will meet UEFA's diverse requirements – speaking to, for example, stadium quality, security, special laws and branding (see e.g., UEFA, 2017) – we can observe how UEFA according to Włoch (2013) has become a 'global governor' who, despite its status as a non-state actor, has the power to shape the interests of nation-states and corporations within the global order.

As Kennedy (2017) reminds us, because one key incentive for UEFA is to ensure that the Euros become a media spectacle that preserves its attractiveness for media corporations and business partners, this means that UEFA places strict conditions on aspiring hosts, and that its growing power coming from 'its wider role to administer and control the use of elite football as a medium to attract capital flows from global corporations and nation-states' (pp. 357–358). In that sense, the interdependent relationships between UEFA and (potential) host countries are perhaps best summarized by the following quote:

> If a state wants to use a sports event for what it perceives as its best interests, whether it be nation building, infrastructural development, or a showcase effect, it must adhere to the conditions set, authoritatively and arbitrarily, by the international sports federation, that is, to sign the restrictive guarantees attached to the bid application. At the same time, the state is completely excluded from the negotiations, as this is deemed a matter between a national football federation and its superior organization. Once a state gets the right to organize the event, the federation starts to act on the guarantees that require legal and institutional transformation of the state.
>
> (Włoch, 2013: 307)

Thus, there are three main departure points that may be extracted from the conceptualization of UEFA as a 'global governor' within the wider context of events' political economy. First, with respect to international relations, this reveals the rescaling of power that has occurred within the international system after the Second World War, which is demonstrated by how entities *lacking* traditional state-defining powers can remain influential actors globally whilst simultaneously relying on states for territories to host events (Giulianotti and Robertson, 2012). Essentially, this speaks to how elite sport remains a field in which reconfigurations of the global order are reinforced or enacted (Włoch, 2013) and how UEFA's power stretches beyond its superior position over national football federations (Garcia et al., 2011).

Second, the discussion reaffirms, in a socio-historical context, how the European Championships have evolved from its modest beginnings into a highly commercialized and politicized spectacle whose attraction has concretized UEFA's role in world football and beyond. One of UEFA's main 'trump cards' is the ability to appoint mega-event hosts (ibid.: 303). This again provides the organization with degrees of power to shape or influence state's actions and the guarantees they make.

Finally, however, these power relations can be contested: states could opt to *not* bid for an event. In the wider mega-event context, the guarantees that states must provide to sport's governing bodies to secure hosting rights have been cited by some as one of the reasons why some host countries in recent years have withdrawn their interest in mega-event hosting rights (see Chapter 5). This again underscores power dynamics inherent in mega-event staging, as some countries consider the action of providing sport's governing bodies required guarantees (thus, degrees of influence and power) as a risky undertaking when considered with the potential social, material and economic gains that could be made from event hosting.

To summarize, this section has focused on two central actors that are necessary to engage with in order to understand the organizational parametres of the European Championships. As argued, by drawing upon Włoch's (2013) theoretical analysis of UEFA as a 'global governor', we can understand not just the organization's position in the international system, but this also helps us understand the power relations and trade-offs that exist between the key actors located around each European Championships and its bidding and planning stages.

Conclusion

The selection of an expanded multinational hosting format for Euro 2020 was, reportedly, explained by UEFA's desire to commemorate the Euros' 60th anniversary (Lee Ludvigsen, 2022). Perhaps accurately, the geographically enlarged format reflected the EU's enlargement and the wider history of the European Championships, which – following its foundation – is much characterized by its continual expansion in terms of competing teams, geography, and commercial activities, including sponsorship, branding and marketing.

This chapter first examined the emergence of the European Championships, which can be traced back to the post-war era of Europe when the tournament was founded in 1958 and first staged in 1960. Second, this chapter has examined the academic literature surrounding the Euros, the event's commercialization and the key actors that are situated within the wider 'football field' (Giulianotti and Robertson, 2012). In order to understand the consistent expansion of the European Championships, to a point where some suggest that the tournament is in direct competition with the

World Cup, this chapter argues that it is highly necessary to understand the more general processes at play speaking to the commercialization of sport and UEFA's concretized role in the worlds of sport and politics as a 'global governor' (Włoch, 2013), which also translates into the European and global marketplaces. Moreover, the chapter highlights that the continued expansion of the Euros concurrently gives life to a myriad of pressing questions that deserve serious attention, and this sport mega-event is undeniably clearly ready for further sociological analysis which recognizes and investigates its roles and positions within the fields of international and European politics, consumer cultures and, as the next chapters focus on specifically, the (new) media and digital practices emerging in relation to the competition.

References

Boykoff J (2014) *Celebration Capitalism and the Olympic Games*. London: Routledge.

Boykoff J (2016) *Power Games: A Political History of the Olympics*. London: Verso.

Chadwick S and Widdop P (2021) Euro 2020 – A football tournament where the big players come from China and the US. *The Conversation*. Available at: https://theconversation.com/euro-2020-a-football-tournament-where-the-big-players-come-from-china-and-the-us-162622 (accessed 05/2022).

Chatzigianni E (2018) Global sport governance: Globalizing the globalized. *Sport in Society* 21(9): 1454–1482.

Cornelissen S (2007) Crafting legacies: The changing political economy of global sport and the 2010 FIFA World Cup™. *Politikon* 34(3): 241–259.

Doidge M, Claus R, Gabler J, Irving R, Millward P and Silvério J (2019) The impact of international football events on local, national and transnational fan cultures: A critical overview. *Soccer & Society* 20(5): 711–720.

Eick V (2011) 'Secure our profits!' The FIFA in Germany 2006. In: C Bennett and K Haggerty (eds.) *Security Games. Surveillance and Control at Mega-Events*. New York: Routledge, pp. 87–102.

Garcia B, Niemann A and Grant W (2011) Conclusion. In: A Niemann, B Garcia and W Grant (eds.) *The Transformation of European Football: Towards the Europeanisation of the National Game*. Manchester: Manchester University Press, pp. 239–261.

Gilchrist P, Holden R and Millward P (2015) Special section introduction: The political sociologies of sport. *Sociological Research Online* 20(2): 141–144.

Giulianotti R (1995) Football and the politics of carnival: An ethnographic study of Scottish fans in Sweden. *International Review for the Sociology of Sport* 30(2): 191–220.

Giulianotti R (2002) Supporters, followers, fans, and flaneurs: A taxonomy of spectator identities in football. *Journal of Sport and Social Issues* 26(1): 25–46.

Giulianotti R (2005) Sport spectators and the social consequences of commodification: Critical perspectives from Scottish football. *Journal of Sport and Social Issues* 29(4): 386–410.

Giulianotti R, Armstrong G, Hales G and Hobbs D (2015) Sport mega-events and public opposition: A sociological study of the London 2012 Olympics. *Journal of Sport and Social Issues* 39(2): 99–119.

Giulianotti R and Numerato D (2018) Global sport and consumer culture: An introduction. *Journal of Consumer Culture* 18(2): 229–240.

Giulianotti R and Robertson R (2012) Mapping the global football field: A sociological model of transnational forces within the world game. *The British Journal of Sociology* 63(2): 216–240.

Grix J and Lee D (2013) Soft power, sports mega-events and emerging states: The lure of the politics of attraction. *Global Society* 27(4): 521–536.

Hagemann A (2010) From the stadium to the fan zone: Host cities in a state of emergency. *Soccer & Society* 11(6): 723–736.

Horne J (2010) Material and representational legacies of sports mega-events: The case of the UEFA EURO™ football championships from 1996 to 2008. *Soccer & Society* 11(6): 854–866.

Kassimeris C (2017) Football in Europe: Apolitical UEFA plays politics with football. In: J Hughson, K Moore, R Spaaij and JA Maguire (eds.) *Routledge Handbook of Football Studies*. London: Routledge, pp. 434–444.

Kennedy P (2017) Using Habermas to crack the European football championships. *Sport in Society* 20(3): 355–368.

Klauser F (2011) The exemplification of 'fan zones': Mediating mechanisms in the reproduction of best practices for security and branding at Euro 2008. *Urban Studies* 48(15): 3202–3219.

Kossakowski R (2019) Euro 2012, the 'civilizational leap' and the 'supporters United' programme: A football mega-event and the evolution of fan culture in Poland. *Soccer & Society* 20(5): 729–743.

Lauss G and Szigetvari A (2010) Governing by fun: EURO 2008 and the appealing power of fan zones. *Soccer & Society* 11(6): 737–747.

Law A (2014) Playing with tension: National charisma and disgrace at Euro 2012. *Soccer & Society* 15(2): 203–221.

Lawrence S and Crawford C (eds.) (2018) *Digital Football Cultures: Fandom, Identities and Resistance*. London: Routledge.

Lee Ludvigsen JA (2020) The 'troika of security': Merging retrospective and futuristic 'risk' and 'security' assessments before Euro 2020. *Leisure Studies* 39(6): 844–858.

Lee Ludvigsen JA (2021a) Mega-events, expansion and prospects: Perceptions of Euro 2020 and its 12-country hosting format. *Journal of Consumer Culture*: 1–19.

Lee Ludvigsen JA (2021b) Between security and festivity: The case of fan zones. *International Review for the Sociology of Sport* 56(2): 233–251.

Lee Ludvigsen JA (2022) *Sport Mega-Events, Security and Covid-19: Securing the Football World*. Oxon and New York: Routledge.

Maguire J and Poulton EK (1999) European identity politics in Euro 96: Invented traditions and national habitus codes. *International Review for the Sociology of Sport* 34(1): 17–29.

Marivoet S (2006) UEFA Euro 2004™ Portugal: The social construction of a sports mega-event and spectacle. *The Sociological Review* 54(2): 127–143.

Millward P (2010) The limits to cosmopolitanism': English football fans at Euro 2008. In: D Burdsey (ed.) *Race, Ethnicity and Football: Persisting Debates and Emergent Issues*. London: Routledge, pp. 163–174.

Millward P, Lee Ludvigsen JA and Sly J (2022) *Sport and Crime: Towards a Critical Criminology of Sport*. London: Routledge.

Mittag J and Legrand B (2010) Towards a Europeanization of football? Historical phases in the evolution of the UEFA European Football Championship. *Soccer & Society* 11(6): 709–722.

O'Brien J (2021) *Euro Summits: The Story of the UEFA European Championships 1960 to 2021*. Pitch Publishing.

Olsson L-C (2011) Decisive moments in UEFA. In: H. Gammelsæter and B. Senaux (eds.) *The Organisation and Governance of Top Football Across Europe: An Institutional Perspective*. New York: Routledge, pp. 17–31.

Pearson G (2012) Dirty Trix at Euro 2008: Brand protection, ambush marketing and intellectual property theft at the European Football Championships. *Entertainment and Sports Law Journal* 10(1): 1–12.

Petersen-Wagner R, Filho AR, Damiani C, et al. (2018) CONMEBOL – South American confederation of football. In: S Chadwick, D Parnell, P Widdop, et al. (eds.) *Routledge Handbook of Football Business and Management*. London: Routledge.

Poulton E (2004) Mediated patriot games: The construction and representation of national identities in the British television production of Euro'96. *International Review for the Sociology of Sport* 39(4): 437–455.

Rahman M and Lockwood S (2011) How to 'use your Olympian': The paradox of athletic authenticity and commercialization in the contemporary Olympic Games. *Sociology* 45(5): 815–829.

Rek-Woźniak M and Woźniak W (2020) BBC's documentary 'Stadiums of Hate' and manufacturing of the news: Case study in moral panics and media manipulation. *Journal of Sport and Social Issues* 44(6): 515–533.

Roche M (2000) *Mega-Events and Modernity: Olympics and Expos in the Growth of Global Culture*. London: Routledge.

Statista (2021) *Number of Official Sponsors at the UEFA EURO Soccer Championship from 2008 to 2020, by Category*. Available at: www.statista.com/statistics/254406/number-of-official-sponsors-at-the-uefa-euro-soccer-championship/ (accessed 05/2022).

Statista (2022) *UEFA European Championships Revenue from 1992 to 2020*. Available at: www.statista.com/statistics/279103/uefa-euro-revenue/ (accessed 05/2022).

Tsoukala A (2009) *Football Hooliganism in Europe: Security and Civil Liberties in the Balance*. Basingstoke: Palgrave Macmillan.

UEFA (2013) *Women's Competitions*. Available at: www.uefa.com/MultimediaFiles/Download/Women/General/01/99/05/49/1990549_DOWNLOAD.pdf (accessed 30/05/2022).

UEFA (2017) *Euro 2024: Tournament Requirements*. Available at: www.uefa.com/multimediafiles/download/officialdocument/uefaorg/regulations/02/46/30/61/2463061_download.pdf (accessed 30/05/2022).

UEFA (2022a) *Women's Euro History*. Available at: www.uefa.com/womenseuro/history/ (accessed 30/05/2022).

UEFA (2022b) *UEFA Euro History*. Available at: www.uefa.com/uefaeuro/history/ (accessed 30/05/2022).

UEFA (n.d.) *UEFA and the European Union*. Available at: www.uefa.com/insideuefa/stakeholders/european-union/ (accessed 30/05/2022).

Vonnard P (2014) A competition that shook European football: The origins of the European Champion Clubs' Cup, 1954–1955. *Sport in History* 34(4): 595–619.

Vonnard P (2020) *Creating a United Europe of Football: The Formation of UEFA (1949–1961)*. Switzerland: Springer.

Vonnard P and Quin G (2017) Did South America foster European football?: Transnational influences on the continentalization of FIFA and the creation of UEFA, 1926–1959. *Sport in Society* 20(10): 142.

Weiss TG (2000) Governance, good governance and global governance: Conceptual and actual challenges. *Third World Quarterly* 21(5): 795–814.

Wise N and Lee Ludvigsen JA (2022) Uniting, disuniting and reuniting: Towards a 'United' 2026. *Sport in Society* 25(4): 837–846.

Włoch R (2013) UEFA as a new agent of global governance: A case study of relations between UEFA and the Polish Government against the background of the UEFA EURO 2012. *Journal of Sport and Social Issues* 37(3): 297–311.

Włoch R (2020) Two dynamics of globalization in the context of a sports mega-event: The case of UEFA EURO 2012 in Poland. *Globalizations* 17(1): 45–59.

3 Old media in new media spaces
Twitter

Introduction

It is undeniable that sport mega-events are already part of the cultural fabric of billions of people around the world, to the point it comes to organize our lives and our sense of belonging to more local (e.g., *national*) or larger spaces (e.g., *Europe*) (Mittag and Legrand, 2010; Crolley and Hand, 2002). As we previously discussed in Chapter 2, sport mega-events are largely mediated experiences of 'celebration capitalism' (Boykoff, 2014), and imagining them without the presence of *mass commercial media* might be just inconceivable (Horne and Manzenreiter, 2006). In a way, it is possible to argue that originally, what made those sporting events 'mega' was their space and time diffusions through the different traditional media formats such as TV, radio and print press (e.g., magazines, newspapers). Therefore, akin to what Boorstin (1961) conceptualized as *pseudo-events*, most of our experiences of the Euros are conditioned by how they are framed by media at large (see Goffmann, 1986 for a discussion on framing) to an extreme position where we can argue that they are now '*media events*' (see Dayan and Katz, 1992). Thus, as predominantly *media events*, the Euros are created and organized for the purposes of commercial media's monetization strategies of connecting advertisers to audiences. Notwithstanding, a less *pessimistic* view of those mediated spectacles might take the position by Deuze (2011), who argues that experiences happen *in* media – rather than *through* or *for* – therefore implying that the Euros as the event, the frame narratives by journalists and other media professionals and our cultural consumption practices as football fans exist *in* the different media formats that are used to bridge the space and time distances of all key actors.

Consequently, if we aspire to provide a sociological analysis of the Euros, it becomes paramount to understand how those events exist *in* the different media formats that are available for the different actors to connect with. This becomes even more relevant especially after the *digital revolution* (see

DOI: 10.4324/9781003359098-3

Negroponte, 1995), when scarcity of content and abundance of attention is substituted by an abundance of content – or media platforms – and a scarcity of attention (Hutchins and Rowe, 2009, 2012). Hence, this chapter seeks to unpack the *novel* symbiotic relationship between media and sport by looking at specifically how two traditional British media organizations who were the TV rights holders of Euro 2020 (staged in 2021) used Twitter as a convergent platform (see Jenkins, 2006).

Conceptualization: sport and media – a symbiotic relationship

To understand the current symbiotic relationship between sport and media that is governed by the *algorithm logic of platforms*, it is important to initially look at the historical roots of those involved actors. As Hobsbawm (1983) argued, both professional sport – in our case football – and commercial media are part of the invented traditions of *European* modernity, evolving alongside other modern institutions such as national culture, education and military, and in particular the overarching structure of the nation-state (see Chernilo, 2007).

The pursuit by commercial media for appealing content that attracted masses and belonged to the popular imagination found its ideal match in the figure of the modern sport – and particularly football in the British Isles (see Mason, 1980) – with its own rhythmic calendar that provided real drama to the audiences in a continual *series* format (see Guttmann, 1978; Rowe, 2004; Jackson, 2013). At the same time, whilst commercial media was satisfied by providing a content that entertained and captivated the attention of masses and thus could be sold to advertisers, public broadcasting media such as the BBC in the UK were also concerned with educating and informing its audience (BBC, 2022), therefore generating and informing a shared cultural citizenship (see Ramon and Rojas-Torrijos, 2021). In a certain way, those three *separate* entities – commercial media, the nation-state in public broadcasting media and professional sport – converged in their path to a point where it becomes impossible to separate one from another, forming the traditional triad symbiotic relationship of Media-Sport-Nation (Rowe, 2004; Hutchins and Rowe, 2012).

Traditional media such as print and radio were integral part of the *nationalization* processes that took place in Europe during the late 1800s and early 1900s – and in a later stage, TV – as they afforded a unifying narrative for imagined communities to sustain and reinforce themselves (Anderson, 2006). In addition, football as true popular cult provided 'common ground for conversation between virtually any two male workers in England or

Scotland' (Hobsbawm, 1983: 289), to a point in which 'the imagined community of millions seems more real as a team of eleven named people. The individual, even the one who only cheers, becomes a symbol of his nation himself' (Hobsbawm, 1992: 143). Therefore, it is uncomplicated to conceive the reasons why both football and commercial or public media as by-products of a specific period of *European* modernization (1875–1915) were geographically bounded to borders of the nation-states, and more specifically how the frame narratives employed by the media sought to reinforce the *zero-sum game* of Imperial competition between those nation-states (see Chernilo, 2007).

As such, every four years the Euros as an international competition between nation-states become a central cultural element for public broadcasting and commercial media to reinforce identity politics to more local or larger *identities*. As Bernstein (2007) showed in terms of the representation of Israel's aspirations to qualify for Euro 2000, different Israeli media sought to draw parallels between the history of the nation-state itself and its footballing position in the world, and how, in the face of its loss to Denmark, this represented an apparent moral decay of Israeli society. Moreover, Vincent and Harris (2014) showed how the Euro 2012 was used to frame *Englishness* by two of the largest British tabloids – *The Sun* and the *Daily Mirror* – in relation to a nostalgic past by idealizing what it meant to be English (e.g., displaying courage, fortitude, discipline in the face of adversities). Those narratives are commonly used in conjunction with their *negative* opposite by putting this idealized identity in contrast with other *national* or *European* identities in a *we* versus *them* frame, as both Vincent and Harris (2014) showed in terms of print press, Poulton (2004) analysed in terms of TV and Euro 1996 and Turskoy (2020) showed in terms of creation of a Turkish identity by the British press during Euro 2016 and Euro 2004 qualifying matches.

It can be said that *historical* (nostalgic and invented) national stereotypes are the backbone of the *we* versus *them* frame, as Maguire and Poulton (1999) analysed in relation to British newspaper coverage of Euro 1996, to a point in which old belligerent tensions resurface as during the England and Germany semi-final game in 1996 (Maguire et al., 1999). On the other hand, some media frames also provided narratives that *united* the different nation-states, such as with Euronews reporting during the Euro 2012 (Law, 2014) or when Irish fans were lionized by foreign and local media for their apparent friendliness during Euro 2016 in France (O'Boyle and Kearns, 2019). Those *unifying* narratives also took place in opposition to the European Union, as in the case of Austrian press during the period of Euro 2008, and the *horizontal* solidarity between Austrians and the Irish people (Karner, 2010).

Either *antagonizing* via 'we versus them' or *conciliating* via horizontal solidarities against others, those frames are still deeply reliant on the nation-state. This geographically-*confined* media as a byproduct of nation-state formations still has its repercussions today as broadcasting rights to Euros – or other sport mega-events – are still commercially based within those territories. For instance, the recent Euro 2020 was commercialized to 229 territories including in-flight entertainment, providing both live and delayed matches, comprehensive highlights and digital coverage to right holders (UEFA, 2021).

In the UK, the BBC and ITV shared the TV rights to broadcast the event live (UEFA, 2015), and allegedly paid UEFA £150 million for rights that also included Euro 2016 in the package (see SportBusinessMedia, 2015). Whilst BBC and ITV are free-to-air TV channels in the UK and thus can have a wider reach in terms of audience, they differ substantially in the way they are funded, as BBC as a national broadcaster is primarily sustained by the television licence fee (over 74% of their income) (BBC, 2021), whilst the broadcasting division of ITV plc (public listed company) relies on subscription and advertising revenues (ITV, 2021). Nonetheless, whilst both predominantly operate as TV channels, in a media industry that is characterized by convergence (Thorburn and Jenkins, 2004; Jenkins, 2006; Jenkins et al., 2013) it is expected that they utilize other digital platforms such as Twitter to either draw attention to their TV live broadcast, or to provide *live* commentary with short clips of main actions of the games.

Their presence on those digital platforms can be seen through McQuail and Deuze's (2020) argument with regards to new media's reverberations on forms of identity formation by concurrently generating spaces for integration and disintegration (e.g., polarization) that *disregard* the borders of the modern nation-state. Because of the underdetermination of the Internet, as Poster (1999) contends, new media such as Twitter transgress the limits of traditional broadcasting by enabling many-to-many communication, dislocating the communicative action away from the territorialized nation-state, and ultimately providing instantaneous global contact between its users. As such, media transformations due to digitalization, and particularly related to the Internet's technological affordances, can be read in conjunction with the current platformization of society (van Dijck et al., 2018), and more specifically how this platformization has impacted the cultural industry of media and sport (Poell et al., 2022). As Nieborg and Poell (2018) argue, modes of news production, distribution and monetization become contingent to platforms, so that news organizations, like ITV and BBC in our case, are considered complementors and become *dependent* on the economic logics of platforms (see also Srnicek, 2017; Murthy, 2017; van Dijck et al., 2018).

Therefore, to understand how BBC and ITV's practices existed *on* Twitter during Euro 2020, it is important to acknowledge both the impacts of the Internet (Poster, 1999) and of platformization (van Dijck et al., 2018; Poell et al., 2022). The question that remains is, if both processes and technology have the *power* to ultimately *transform* this historical sedimented symbiotic relationship between media, sport and the nation-state, or if because of the very nature of inter-nation competition and broadcasting rights' arrangements, what we are witnessing are just *accommodations* in this novel medium.

Hence, the next section examines these transformative practices using Euro 2020 as an example. Euro 2020 was hosted across 11 different countries during the Covid-19 pandemic. Subsequently, this impeded the mobilities of fans travelling to the fan zones and stadiums. As UEFA (n.d.) acknowledged, this enhanced the importance of social media channels, second screen use and content creation. Whilst the significance of Euro 2020 on social media is underlined by the 279 million impressions (between 7 June and 18 July) on UEFA's social media channels, we remain concerned here with the nature of broadcasters' adaption to social media in a time where Twitter undoubtedly is one key space of the Euros and its broadcasting.

Twitter: a space for the Euros

The microblogging platform Twitter is characterized by its *free*-to-use, multicasting (many-to-many networked connections), interactive and multimedia content that encourages users to constantly update their *status* (e.g., tweet), conforming to its core agnostic approach to content (Murthy, 2017). Therefore Twitter, like other social media platforms such as YouTube, Facebook, Instagram, Reddit, Snapchat and TikTok does not create content itself, but relies on the constant creation of content by complementors, be they *common* users or *institutional* users such as BBC and ITV. As an infrastructure platform, Twitter controls the multisided market by acting as the sole matchmaker between advertisers, common and professional users who *tweet* and content partners who provide videos for increasing reach and engagement around global events (see Twitter, 2021: 7), therefore directing its business model towards the commodification of user attention through personalized advertising based on big data (van Dijck et al., 2018). Twitter (2021) counts 217 million average monetizable daily active usage (mDAU),[1] of which 179 million are based internationally (outside the USA), with an annual advertising revenue of over 4.5 billion US Dollars (a 40% increase from 2020). Consequently, we can argue that Twitter, as a place, matters for those over 200 million daily users who are constantly *prosuming* content in the platform, becoming central in public self-expression during real-time events such as the Euros.

In terms of sport, Twitter is conceived as a medium for telepresence (Hutchins, 2011; Petersen-Wagner, 2022) where users can be together whilst physically distant apart, thus disrupting the sport communication ecosystem (Pegoraro, 2014) by the reverberation power of tweets (Billings, 2014) that can bypass the editorial logic of media gatekeepers (Petersen-Wagner, 2022). As O'Hallarn et al. (2018) demonstrate, whilst hashtags provide a common *space* for discussion around a particular topic and therefore resemble the public sphere conceived by Habermas (1991), what may be seen is that users are not fully engaging in back-and-forth debates, nor that *common* users constantly have prominence in networks formed around particular hashtags (Yan et al., 2019; see Petersen-Wagner, 2022 for a distinct finding).

In terms of our case study for this chapter – as we alluded to in Chapter 1 – we scraped tweets between 10 June and 12 July 2021 from @BBCSport and @itvfootball using R and then automatically cleaned the data to keep only the tweets using #bbceuro2020 and #uefaeuro hashtags respectively, leaving us with 1,743 tweets for BBC and 1,306 tweets for ITV.[2] To complement our analyses, we have also collected all tweets using #bbceuro2020 hashtag between the same dates, formulating a database of 115,975 tweets.

Initially, what we can observe from Figures 3.1 and 3.2 is how the distribution of tweets by the two media organizations reflects in particular the participation of the English national team during the Euros and, to a lesser extent, the Welsh and Scottish teams. For instance, on 12 June Wales drew with Switzerland in their first group stage game (@BBCSport – 72 tweets; @itvfootball – 35 tweets), then on 13 June England beat Croatia (@BBCSport – 85 tweets; @itvfootball – 69 tweets) and on 14 June Scotland lost to the Czech Republic (@BBCSport – 80 tweets; @itvfootball – 52 tweets). Interestingly, the tweets from the day Wales played received more likes than the other two days, which can be seen in these figures as it was included in Cluster 5 (higher number of likes). Unsurprisingly, another day in Cluster 5 in terms of likes for both ITV and BBC and having an above-average number of tweets was the final day between England and Italy on 11 July. As for content, as we have alluded to previously, both ITV and BBC sought to provide *live* commentary of the games being played, with both updates in score and short clips, and to draw audiences to their live TV broadcast (linear or digital via BBC iPlayer or ITV Hub). In this manner, we note how both media companies demonstrated a *dependency* (Poell et al., 2022) on Twitter in terms of distribution and capturing audiences to their main *medium* (TV). For that reason, it is possible to argue that as a non-rival type of content (tweets with short clips highlights and *live* commentaries), the platform was used complementary (Gantz and Lewis, 2014) to that of other media, such as TV or radio for the BBC, or to other programmes within their organization.

@bbcsport (#bbceuro2020)

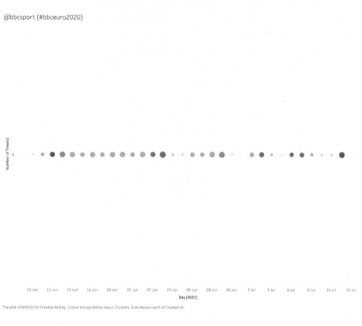

Figure 3.1 @BBCSport (Tweets per Day/Likes)

@itvfootball

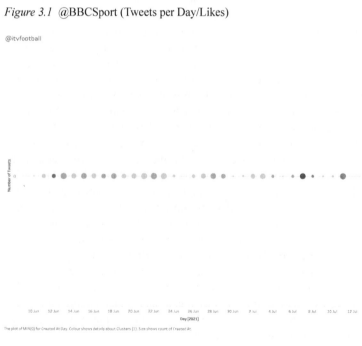

Figure 3.2 @itvfootball (Tweets per Day/Likes)

The last point becomes more evident when looking at Figures 3.3 and 3.4 in terms of who the users were that both BBC and ITV mentioned in their tweets. This is particularly striking for the BBC, as their top eight mentioned users were the TV show 'Match of the Day', their podcast and music platform BBC Sounds, their digital video-on-demand service BBC iPlayer, their TV channels BBC One and BBC Two, their online news portal BBC Sport and radio station BBC 5 Live. This content strategy by the BBC finds resonance in what Jenkins (2006) and Jenkins et al. (2013) discuss in terms of convergence and spreadable content. Nevertheless, whilst Jenkins et al. (2013) emphasize the notion of grassroots participation in the spread of content – which also finds resonance on Poster's (1999) analysis of the underdetermination of the Internet in terms of many-to-many networked communication – what we found from this analysis is that neither BBC nor ITV mention any *common* user in their tweets. Not only they do not mention *common* users, but they do also not engage in any true dialogue with their audiences, as there are almost no *replies* to users (ITV replied only twice to current English players, whilst there were no replies from the BBC). In a way, whilst the affordances of the Internet and of Twitter as a platform rest on multicasting and network interactions, both BBC and ITV

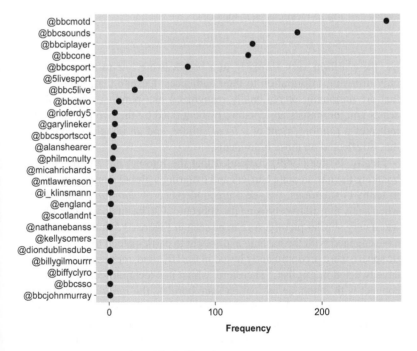

Figure 3.3 Top 25 mentions (@BBCSport)

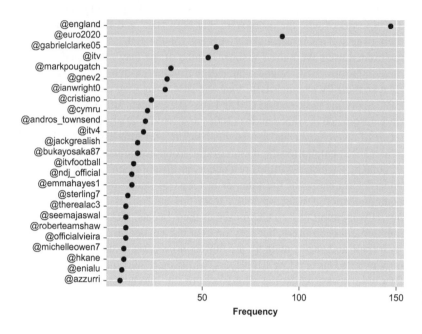

Figure 3.4 Top 25 mentions (@itvfootball)

use the platform very similarly to a broadcasting one-to-many model by only diffusing information to their audiences. Despite that, *public figures* that are nationally or regionally recognized like pundits, former players, artists and journalists are commonly mentioned by the two profiles, which indicates a reinforcement of a *local* culture, and an imagined community that is reflected on those individuals.

Finally, Poster (1999) contended that the Internet has the potential for breaking the nation-state barriers and fostering a global community. Whilst, in terms of mentions, we see a preponderance of *national public figures*, when analysing all tweets using the #bbceuro2020 hashtag, what we observe was a very similar picture. As can be seen in Figures 3.5 and 3.6, users who have engaged with the hashtag and sought to participate in this form of public sphere were predominantly based in the UK[3] and, more specifically, they have tweeted in English.[4] Therefore, whilst it is technologically possible to connect with others across nation-state borders, the *reality* is that because of the way broadcasting rights are commercialized, users tend to engage with their *local* (national) rights holder. This argument is further reinforced by the very nature of communication (*communicare* in Latin derives from

Figure 3.5 Map of #bbceuro2020 users/language (Cities)

© 2022 Mapbox © OpenStreetMap

Map based on Longitude (generated) and Latitude (generated). Colour shows details about Lang. Size shows details about User Loaction. The view is filtered on Latitude (generated) and Longitude (generated). The Latitude (generated) filter keeps non-Null values only. The Longitude (generated) filter keeps non-Null values only.

Figure 3.6 Map of #bbceuro2020 users/language (NUT Regions)

communis, which means to make common or share) that rests on a shared and common language that is spoken and written by all participants. As Hobsbawn (1996) argued, the idea of an idealized 'imagined community' bound to the nation-state included notions of homogeneity in terms of ethnicity, culture and particularly language. Nevertheless, it is important to acknowledge, as Hobsbawn (1996) does, that this aspired-towards homogeneity of the *creation* of nation-states is impossible to achieve without ruthless expulsion of individuals who speak other languages, especially in today's world which is characterized by an increased mobility of people (see also Sheller and Urry, 2006). Whilst English was the preponderant language in those tweets using the #bbceuro2020 hashtag, we found tweets in 18 other identified languages,[5] in addition to some which were undefined.

In sum, whilst digital transformations and particularly the advent of the Internet and the current platformization of cultural industries might have the power of generating profound changes to the way sport is *prosumed* in media, what we encountered were small accommodations to the traditional nationally-bounded symbiotic relationship between media and sport. Therefore, we contend that researchers and commentators need to be prudent when highlighting the impacts of digital technologies in sport and media and be attentive to both patterns of changes and continuities found *in* those new technologies and different media platforms.

Conclusion

As we sought to highlight in this chapter, the Euros as a 'media event' (Dayan and Katz, 1992) happens *in* the different media that frames our experience of the event. Whilst these frames in the past predominantly existed in traditional media such as radio, TV and print, because of the current digitalization and platformization, our experiences are now shaped in the multitude of media that we – as users – have access to. As one of the most used social media platforms, and specifically one whose primarily affordance rests on communal commenting on *real-time events*, Twitter provides an ideal case for comprehending how the Euros exist in this new media ecology that is characterized by content abundance and attention scarcity (Hutchins and Rowe, 2009, 2012).

Whereas the Internet and other new media technologies have the power to revolutionize the sedimented symbiotic relationship between media and sport, which traces its history to a specific time in European modernization, what we uncovered with our analysis of Euro 2020 on Twitter and subsequently argue is that the configuration of this new relationship carries more patterns of continuities rather than complete structural breaks, as in a revolution.

Hence, whereas this chapter ties into the extant work on the nexus between the Euros and the media (Maguire and Poulton, 1999; Maguire et al., 1999), it is critical for researchers and commentators to be attentive to how practices on new media platforms are still conditioned to *old* historical routines, and to other external social, political and legal frameworks, such as the broadcasting rights arrangements that are based on the borders of nation-states. Furthermore, as we unpack further in the next chapter focusing on video-sharing platform YouTube, it is paramount that different platforms are not considered monolithically, as they not only have evolved distinctively over their existence, but the practices within them have also been transformed into different directions.

Notes

1 As Twitter (2021: 42) states: 'We define mDAU as people, organizations or other accounts who logged in or were otherwise authenticated and accessed Twitter on any given day through twitter.com, Twitter applications that are able to show ads, or paid Twitter products, including subscriptions'.
2 Euro 2020 took place between 11 June and 11 July 2021.
3 The analysis is based on user declared location on their profile (user_location on Twitter API); as users can add any information, this is an approximation and might not reflect their true geographical location when tweeting.
4 According to Twitter API documentation, language (lang on Twitter API) detection is a best-effort.
5 CS = Czech; CY = Welsh; DA = Danish; DE = German; EN = English; ES = Spanish; ET = Estonian; FI = Finnish; FR = French; HT = Haitian; IN = Indonesian; IT = Italian; NL = Dutch; PL = Polish; PT = Portuguese; RO = Romanian; TL = Tagalog; TR = Turkish.

References

Anderson B (2006) *Imagined Communities*. London: Verso.
BBC (2021) *BBC Group Annual Report and Accounts 2020/2021*. Available at: https://downloads.bbc.co.uk/aboutthebbc/reports/annualreport/2020-21.pdf (accessed 01/06/2022).
BBC (2022) *Mission, Values and Public Purposes*. Available at: www.bbc.com/aboutthebbc/governance/mission (accessed 31/05/2022).
Bernstein A (2007) 'Running nowhere': National identity and media coverage of the Israeli Football Team's attempt to qualify for Euro 2000. *Israel Affairs* 13(3): 653–664.
Billings A (2014) Power in the reverberation: Why Twitter matters, but not the way most believe. *Communication & Sport* 2(2): 107–112.
Boorstin D (1961) *The Image: A Guide to Pseudo-Events in America*. London: Vintage.
Boykoff J (2014) *Celebration Capitalism and the Olympic Games*. London: Routledge.
Chernilo D (2007) *A Social Theory of the Nation-State: The Political Forms of Modernity Beyond Methodological Nationalism*. London: Routledge.

Crolley L and Hand D (2002) *Football, Europe and the Press*. London: Routledge.

Dayan D and Katz E (1992) *Media Events: The Live Broadcasting of History*. Cambridge, MA: Harvard University Press.

Deuze M (2011) Media life. *Media, Culture & Society* 33(1): 137–148.

Gantz W and Lewis N (2014) Sports on traditional and newer digital media. *Television & New Media* 15(8): 760–768.

Goffman E (1986) *Frame Analysis: An Essay on the Organization of Experience*. Boston: Northeastern University Press.

Guttmann A (1978) *From Ritual to Record: The Nature of Modern Sports*. New York: Columbia University Press.

Habermas J (1991) *The Structural Transformation of the Public Sphere: An Inquiry into a Category of Bourgeois Society*. Cambridge, MA: MIT Press.

Hobsbawm E (1983) Mass-producing traditions: Europe, 1870–1914. In: E. Hobsbawm and T. Ranger (eds.) *The Invention of Tradition*. Cambridge: Cambridge University Press, pp. 263–307.

Hobsbawm E (1992) *Nations and Nationalism since 1780: Programme, Myth, Reality*. Cambridge: Cambridge University Press.

Hobsbawn E (1996) Language, culture, and national identity. *Social Research* 63(4): 1065–1080.

Horne J and Manzenreiter W (2006) An introduction to the sociology of mega-events. *The Sociological Review* 54(2): 1–24.

Hutchins B (2011) The acceleration of media sport culture: Twitter, telepresence and online messaging. *Information, Communication & Society* 14(2): 237–257.

Hutchins B and Rowe D (2009) From broadcast scarcity to digital plenitude. *Television & New Media* 10(4): 354–370.

Hutchins B and Rowe D (2012) *Sport beyond Television: The Internet, Digital Media and the Rise of Networked Media Sport*. London: Routledge.

ITV (2021) *ITV PLC Annual Report and Accounts for the Year Ended 31 December 2021*. Available at: www.itvplc.com/~/media/Files/I/ITV-PLC/documents/reports-and-results/annual-report-2021.pdf (accessed 01/06/2022).

Jackson S (2013) Reflections on communication and sport: On advertising and promotional culture. *Communication & Sport* 1(1–2): 100–112.

Jenkins H (2006) *Convergence Culture: Where Old and New Media Collide*. New York: New York University Press.

Jenkins H, Ford S and Green J (2013) *Spreadable Media: Creating value and Meaning in a Networked Culture*. New York: New York University Press.

Karner C (2010) The uses of the past and European integratrion: Austria between Lisbon, Ireland, and Euro 08. *Identities: Global Studies in Culture and Power* 17(4): 387–410.

Law A (2014) Playing with tension: National charisma and disgrace at Euro 2012. *Soccer & Society* 15(2): 203–221.

Maguire J and Poulton E (1999) European identity politics in Euro 96: Invented traditions and national habitus codes. *International Review for the Sociology of Sport* 34(1): 17–29.

Maguire J, Poulton E and Possamai C (1999) Weltkrieg III?: Media coverage of England versus Germany in Euro 96. *Journal of Sport & Social Issues* 23(4): 439–454.

Mason T (1980) *Association Football and English Society: 1863–1915*. Sussex: The Harvester Press.

McQuail D and Deuze M (2020) *McQuail's Media and Mass Communication Theory*. London: SAGE.

Mittag J and Legrand B (2010) Towards a Europeanization of football? Historical phases in the evolution of the UEFA European Football Championship. *Soccer & Society* 11(6): 709–722.

Murthy D (2017) *Twitter: Social Communication in the Twitter Age*. Cambridge: Polity.

Negroponte N (1995) *Being Digital*. London: Hodder & Stoughton.

Nieborg D and Poell T (2018) The platformization of cultural production: Theorizing the contingent cultural commodity. *New Media & Society* 20(11): 4275–4292.

O'Boyle N and Kearns C (2019) The Greening of Euro 2016: Fan footage, representational tropes, and media lionization of the irish in France. *Television & New Media* 20(1): 96–116.

O'Hallarn B, Shapiro S, Hambrick M, et al. (2018) Sport, Twitter hashtags, and the public sphere: A qualitative test of the phenomenon through a Curt Schilling case study. *Journal of Sport Management* 32(4): 389–400.

Pegoraro A (2014) Twitter as disruptive innovation in sport communication. *Communication & Sport* 2(2): 132–137.

Petersen-Wagner R (2022) The business of FIFA World Cup: Digital and social media. In: S Chadwick, D Parnell, P Widdop, et al. (eds.) *Routledge Handbook of Business of FIFA World Cup*. London: Routledge.

Poell T, Nieborg D and Duffy BE (2022) *Platforms and Cultural Production*. Cambridge: Polity Press.

Poster M (1999) Underdetermination. *New Media & Society* 1(1): 12–17.

Poulton E (2004) Mediated patriotic games: The construction and representation of national identities in the British television production of Euro '96. *International Review for the Sociology of Sport* 39(4): 437–455.

Ramon X and Rojas-Torrijos JL (2021) Public service media, sports and cultural citizenship in the age of social media: An analysis of BBC Sport agenda diversity on Twitter. *International Review for the Sociology of Sport* OnlineFirst: 1–22.

Rowe D (2004) *Sport, Culture and the Media: The Unruly Trinity*. Maidenhead: Open University Press.

Sheller M and Urry J (2006) The new mobilities paradigm. *Environment and planning A* 38(2): 207–226.

SportBusinessMedia (2015) *UEFA Secures Increase from Age-Old BBC/ITV Alliance*. Available at: https://media.sportbusiness.com/2015/10/uefa-secures-increase-from-age-old-bbc-itv-alliance/ (accessed 14/06/2022).

Srnicek N (2017) *Platform Capitalism*. Cambridge: Polity Press.

Thorburn D and Jenkins H (2004) *Rethinking Media Change: The Aesthetics of Transition*. Cambridge, MA: MIT Press.

Turksoy N (2020) 'Roy's Turkish delight': Football, nationalism and the representation of Turkey in the British sports media. *Journalism Practice* 14(4): 499–514.

Twitter (2021) *Fiscal Year 2021 Annual Report*. Available at: https://s22.q4cdn.com/826641620/files/doc_financials/2021/ar/FiscalYR2021_Twitter_Annual_-Report.pdf (accessed 14/06/2022).

UEFA (2015) *BBC and ITV Gain Euro 2016 and 2020 Rights*. Available at: www.uefa.com/uefaeuro/history/news/0253-0d80bb5bf72b-31e63c8834d6-1000--bbc-and-itv-gain-euro-2016-and-2020-rights/ (accessed 01/06/2022).

UEFA (2021) *Where to Watch the UEFA Euro 2020 Final: TV Broadcast Partners, Live Streams*. Available at: www.uefa.com/uefaeuro/history/news/025a-0ec0d02154c8-5fa71e862f15-1000--where-to-watch-euro-2020/ (accessed 01/06/2022).

UEFA (n.d.) *UEFA Euro 2020 Went Viral: A Special Tournament: On the Pitch, and on Social Media*. Available at: https://editorial.uefa.com/resources/0276-157 69ffa5879-a62705924d6d-1000/220225_uefa_euro_2020_goes_viral_20220624112434.pdf?fbclid=IwAR1L3-V2MCoBG5NCN2MDc6znwadasX-1WY6lYwwyJa3_CxA667d97zodPVt8.

van Dijck J, Poell T and de Waal M (2018) *The Platform Society: Public Values in a Connective World*. Oxford: Oxford University Press.

Vincent J and Harris J (2014) 'They think it's all Dover!' Popular newspaper narratives and images about the English football team and (re)presentations of national identity during Euro 2012. *Soccer & Society* 15(2): 222–240.

Yan G, Watanabe N, Shapiro S, et al. (2019) Unfolding the Twitter scene of the 2017 UEFA Champions League Final: Social media networks and power dynamics. *European Sport Management Quarterly* 19(4): 419–436.

4   YouTube as an alternative to TV

Remediating the spectacle

Introduction

As discussed in Chapter 3, conceptualizing professional sport – and particularly football mega-events – as a media spectacle appears to be an unelaborated pleonasm, as its actual configuration and organization are heavily intertwined with commercial and public broadcasting media to a point where, in this symbiotic relationship (see Rowe, 2004), it becomes impossible to distinguish where one starts and the other ends. Notwithstanding, this enmeshed relationship is not more strongly experienced than on what is possibly the most important medium for sport mega-events: television (see Bourdieu, 1998; Chisari, 2006). As Rowe (1996) contends, the relationship between professional sport and television is a mutual love affair – or a match made in heaven (Galily and Tamir, 2014) – where, on one hand, the medium provides technological affordances for reaching geographically dispersed individuals in a live format whilst, on the other, football mega-events provide the much-sought content that can captivate billions around the world and consequently be sold to advertisers.

For instance, staged across 11 countries, Euro 2020 was broadcasted to 229 territories through 494 TV channels (137 unique broadcasters) (UEFA, 2021a). It had a cumulative global audience of 5.2 billion viewers (UEFA, 2021b), whilst the final game between Italy and England had a live audience of 328 million (UEFA, 2021b) – with that figure being over 70% of the European Union's entire population (World Bank, 2022). To put these figures into perspective, the FIFA 2018 Russia Men's World Cup had over 3 billion unique viewers and the final was projected to have over 1 billion as a live audience (FIFA, 2018; Petersen-Wagner, 2022), which demonstrates that whilst the Euros trails behind the men's FIFA World Cup, as a *regional* event it still possesses a sheer global reach in terms of audience and interest (see Chapters 1 and 2).

In spite of that, whilst TV still possesses a position of supremacy in terms of platform selection for moving-images types of content, in a digital media

DOI: 10.4324/9781003359098-4

environment that is characterized by content abundancy and attention scarcity (Hutchins and Rowe, 2009, 2012), other platforms emerge as alternatives for consumption of such content (Petersen-Wagner, 2022). Moreover, it is commonly maintained in media circles that there is a pattern of shorter attention span amongst new generations of consumers (see Newman, 2010), and that Gen-Z and Millennials are more likely to consume *news* from social media platforms (see Statista, 2021; Statista, 2022a), so it is perhaps unsurprising that the 90-minute *live* football match on TV might become less attractive for captivating audiences' full attention (see Statista, 2022b for figures about the decline of the NFL Super Bowl's TV audience).

Considering this, it is important to question how specific social media platforms – and in this chapter we focus on YouTube – are remediating (see Bolter and Grusin, 2000) the most important content in terms of football: the live moving image of a 90-minute game. Thus, to shed light on the remediation practices taking place *on* YouTube in terms of the Euros, this chapter follows with a discussion on the once-centrality of TV as the primary sport medium. Then it focuses on processes of remediation, before finishing with an analysis of 17 Euro 2020 official broadcasters' channels on YouTube (see UEFA, 2021a, for a full list of official broadcasters).[1]

Conceptualization: television, spectacle and remediation

Following the critical theories of Debord (1999), it has become commonplace to align sport (or sport mega-events) to media or television 'spectacles' (see also Dayan and Katz, 1992). Normally, sport mega-events are 'hyped up, and given massive media coverage' (Marivoet, 2006: 136), and their position as spectacles represents 'one of their most important products on the market of cultural consumption' (ibid.: 139). As Pierre Bourdieu (1998) observed in his work on the Olympics, this means that the production of mega-events is characterized by a duplex nature. In his view, mega-events were physically played out in the stadiums, but they also take place as *televised* spectacles on a global level. Yet writing in the late 1990s, Bourdieu's visionary take on mega-events could not, for obvious reasons, account for developments that intensified in the early 2000s which, *inter alia*, saw the mediation of sport mega-events extend beyond television, print media and radio. However, Bourdieu's (1998) emphasis on the double production of mega-events remains relevant and intriguing, serving as a starting point for understanding sport, and particularly the Euros, in a digital age.

Reflecting on the similar cultural circumstances as Bourdieu did in his book in the mid-1990s, and particularly in terms of the extensive mediation through satellite TV of sport mega-events such as the 1980 Moscow and 1984 Los Angeles Olympic Games, Whannel (1985, 1986) showed how television became central for the *production* of sport to a point where it had the power to change culturally embedded configurations both locally (in the United Kingdom) and internationally (in non-*Western* countries). For instance, Whannel (1985: 62) argued that 'television has come to have a major effect on the image people hold of sports and their associated values and ideals', especially by the close association of sport and media that reflected some form of imperialism in terms of practices in producing the media spectacle. As Whannel (1985) showed, already in the 1978 Argentina FIFA World Cup there was a desire for normalizing, under a European standard, the production of images as in the camera angles used for covering the live game, and also in the technology (the PAL colour system rather than the NTSC system adopted in the USA) used to produce such lives images. In this regard, it is possible to link the double production of sport mega-events on television back to the 1970s to geopolitical and businesses' questions, as in the PAL versus NTSC and to a lesser extent SECAM (used in France and within its sphere of influence) *format*-war that had repercussions on sales of equipment both to produce and consume TV. Furthermore, it is interesting to note how football as a media spectacle is historically more in debt to a European entertainment model, whereas the Olympics might follow a more North American model, given the *dominance* of NBC in terms of broadcasting rights investments (see Billings, 2008)

The further penetration of media models and particularly the one prevalent on television in the sport environment meant further spectacularization and glamourization in order to enhance the entertainment value of the sport product and ultimately minimize any potential dullness coming from the actual contest (Whannel, 1986). In a way, the football game watched on television with its close-ups, slow motion replays (Chisari, 2006), commentaries and interviews – and nowadays further data overlays – becomes something different from the one seen in the stadiums (see also Galily, 2014). As Sandvoss (2003) argued, television had ultimately transformed the way games are viewed/watched and experienced by audiences, having far-reaching consequences in both the experience and expectations of consuming the football spectacle *in* media and *in*-situ. These ramifications were global in scope, as Chisari (2006) highlights that – from the late 1960s onwards – television was the key medium through which football's globalization intensified.

Nevertheless, the advanced media penetration into sport was not without concerns, as Rowe (1996) and Whannel (1986) show, especially in terms of more popular sports like football, which historically relied considerably on gate receipts for their economic sustainability. However, football clubs and organizations such as FIFA and UEFA started to see the *benefits* of broadcasting live football games because of the wider diffusion of the images to far-reaching audiences. This in turn allowed them to improve their sponsor-ship earnings either through shirt sponsors (clubs) and/or advertising boards (clubs and competitions organizers) (Rowe, 1996; Whannel, 1986, 1992). This was further expanded through the late 1990s and early 2000s, when the broadcasting rights for major football leagues and tournaments such as the Euros and FIFA World Cups (see Dart, 2014) substantially increased and overtook other forms of income generation (see Chapter 2; Buraimo et al., 2006), in line with a wider liberalization of audio-visual markets in Europe (Garcia et al., 2011).

Nevertheless, whilst television for the past half of the century has domi-nated the sport-media nexus in terms of platform selection, with the current digitalization and platformization in the cultural industries (see Poell et al., 2022), new players have emerged as alternatives for spectacularizing mega-events (see Gantz and Lewis, 2014; Lee Ludvigsen and Petersen-Wagner, 2022). As Briggs and Burke (2020) and Jenkins (2006) argue, it is impor-tant to avoid a simplistic technological determinist position and therefore observe only the *demise* of a particular media technology (e.g. satellite television and/or digital television) but to interrogate what are the *cultural* elements (e.g. socializations) that take place *in* this media. Hence, whilst television as the hard technological artefact might be losing its centrality to other devices such as phones, tablets and computers, and the cultural consumption habits might be more physically atomized – but concurrently metaphysically together (see Petersen-Wagner, 2018; Lee Ludvigsen and Petersen-Wagner, 2022) – the Euros as the content delivered by the different media technologies continue to be central to a ritualistic passion for football that is mostly expressed every four years (Chapter 2).

However, as Briggs and Burke (2020) and Jenkins (2006) contend, the *demise* of one technology does not entail its complete disappearance from the ecology of media, but an accommodation with new and other older technologies in accordance with convergence media environment (see also Thorburn and Jenkins, 2004). Therefore, extending Bourdieu's (1998) observations of the 'double production' of sport mega-events, we can argue that in the current platform society, what is experienced by individuals is a multiplex *production* of meaning that takes place *in* the different media platforms. Consequently, it is possible to argue that the *live* 90-minute game is now repurposed for different media formats to suit those distinct plat-forms, with these platforms being more focused on video (horizontal and/or vertical) (e.g. YouTube, Twitch, Instagram and TikTok), text (e.g. Twitter and Reddit), still image (e.g. Instagram) or voice (e.g. Spotify, Clubhouse and Discord). Furthermore, distinctively to Sandvoss' (2003: 140) argu-ment that '[w]hereas television football is universally available, its con-sumption is nevertheless firmly situated within the domestic sphere', the digital *multiplex* spectacle of football is now firmly inscribed in the current trends of media mobility, exemplified by the anytime/anywhere type of media consumption (see McQuail and Deuze, 2020; Hutchins and Rowe, 2012) that consequently is accelerated (e.g. focus on shorter formats) to fit into *smaller* pieces of leisure time.

As Bolter and Grusin (2000) highlight, in the current convergent digital media environment, the double logic of remediation becomes even more apparent through the ambivalent function media play in our lives, by on one hand *hyper*media*ting* events and on the other creating *im*media*cies*. In a way, more media means less media where, by oversaturating users with content, it ends by providing an experience of *being there* without media. For instance, the juxtaposition of different camera angles, slow motion, VAR and goal-line technologies into a 3-minute YouTube clip serves as a reminder of hypermediation but concurrently provides what almost emerges as an experience of immediacy. The repurposing or remediation of content from one medium to other media – or even within the same medium – becomes a common practice in this ecology of media that is characterized by platform abundance. Nevertheless, it is important to acknowledge that those practices are both economically and aesthetically motivated in order to achieve market dominance (see Bolter and Grusin, 2000). Moreover, whilst it might be easier to conceive how newer media platforms are remediating or repurposing older media formats (e.g. YouTube remediating TV), the processes are not only linear and uni-directional but happen in multiple ways, such as when TV aesthetically borrows from the Web and provides windowed overlays and multiple camera options, or from video games by providing a first-person viewpoint (e.g. head-mounted cameras or chest strap cameras) and the use of bokeh type of shots that resembles videogame cinematics.

Against this backdrop, examining how YouTube is remediating TV through the Euros provides a window not only to understand this side of the coin (newer media remediating older), but it also sheds light on the other side of the coin by revealing the possible directions that TV might take in order to remain an important medium for newer generations.

YouTube: an alternative to TV

Initially conceived as a predominant horizontal video-sharing platform, YouTube was released to the public in 2005 and purchased by Google (now Alphabet Inc.) in 2006 for US$ 1.65 billion (Burgess and Green, 2018). Whilst facing competition from other predominantly vertical video-sharing platforms such as TikTok (ByteDance) and Instagram (Meta), YouTube is still considered the largest video-sharing platform in terms of user base

(Statista, 2022c), having over 100 localized versions in 80 different languages (YouTube, 2022a). Like other platforms, YouTube has metamorphosed over the years, moving from an amateur 'broadcast yourself' model (see Jarret, 2008) to now control the multisided market that still involves amateur creators but also caters to professional and institutional creators, advertisers, media partners and multichannel networks (Burgess and Green, 2018; Bärtl, 2018; Lobato, 2016). The changes within YouTube are not restricted to the business model and monetization strategies it uses (see Ørmen and Gregeresen, 2022), but also encompasses the technological affordances such as the ability to post a video of over 15min or stream entire events (YouTube, 2022b, 2022c), and post Shorts (less than 60s and vertical videos) (YouTube, 2022d). In a similar fashion to Twitter (Chapter 3), whilst YouTube's revenue counts also with YouTube Premium and You-Tube TV subscriptions, the adverts showed to its 2 billion monthly-logged users (YouTube, 2022a) are the primary source of income. The advertisement side of the business contributes with over 10% of its parent company's (Alphabet Inc) annual revenue (Alphabet, 2022), with a sum of US$ 28,845 billion (an increase of around 45% from 2021).

In terms of sport-YouTube nexus, YouTube was historically considered as a primary medium for repurposing and remediating content produced for other media, such as television (Stauff, 2009). Currently, YouTube also acts as a primary medium where *original* content is consumed. For instance, different brands, national and international sporting governing bodies, clubs, fans and media organizations use YouTube to connect directly to their audience, therefore bypassing *traditional gatekeepers* (see Petersen-Wagner, 2022; Petersen-Wagner and Lee Ludvigsen, 2022a, 2022b; Lee Ludvigsen and Petersen-Wagner, 2022; McCarthy, 2021; Checchinato et al., 2015; Rivers and Ross, 2021). In terms of live football broadcasting, whilst other infrastructural platforms such as Amazon and Apple have signed multi-year deals with leagues around the world (*The Guardian*, 2021, 2022; Apple, 2022), YouTube still relies on its media partners to showcase content they have the digital rights for, such as in the case of BT Sport in the UK broadcasting the UEFA Champions League, Europa League, and Conference League finals (*The Guardian*, 2016).

As alluded to, whilst the Euros is a mega-event contested by *regional* nations, its broadcasting deals encompasses the entire world and attract the attention of millions worldwide. Whilst academic analyses in terms of audience commonly favour the primary medium of television, in this chapter we focus on the YouTube channels of 17 different rights holders of Euro 2020 that were based around the world. To collect the metrics of all 17 official playlists, initially we had to access YouTube using virtual private networks (VPNs) to circumvent geoblocking (see Lobato and Meese, 2016; Meese and Podckalicka, 2016) as, similar to television rights deals, digital rights are also commercialized based on nation-states and territories (see Chapter 3 for a discussion on the relationship between nation-state, media and sport). Whilst it is possible to find the official channels of those 17 distinct broadcasters without the use of VPNs, the playlists associated with Euro 2020 are commonly hidden from *foreign* access, meaning that only *local* users can have access to those videos.

As such, whilst YouTube seems to be a single platform, it can be considered as *YouTubes* because of the localized versions that contain restricted content and adverts catered for those localities and audiences. As seen in Table A.1, the 17 official broadcasters had different approaches in terms of creating and remediating content for their Euro 2020 playlists, with the most common approach being uploading shorter videos, and more specifically of the highlights of all 51 games (see also Figure A.2). Nevertheless, whilst most channels focused solely on match highlights, two broadcasters have repurposed other TV content, like when ITV (UK) added pundits' commentaries, pre-matches analyses, players' interviews and videos of fans without any commentary, whilst beIN Sports (France) added post-match interviews with players and managers, highlights of specific players and all teams' presentations before the event started.

In terms of the videos' length, on average across all channels, they had 478s – to put into perspective an entire football game has 5,400s – but there was variance between and within channels, especially on channels that used the latest technological affordances in terms of posting over-15min videos or streaming entire events, such as Optus Sport (Australia), Rai (Italy), SRF Sport (Switzerland) and tvN (South Korea). For instance, Optus Sport had live pre-game *talk shows* and *chat rooms* for build-ups but no highlights on their official playlist, whilst SRF Sport alongside their highlights videos had also streamed, with a delay, entire games under the #Re-Live hashtag. In terms of Rai, instead of remediating television content as with game highlights, the only content available on their playlist was repurposed from Rai Radio 1 broadcasts of the seven Italian games in the tournament, whilst tvN approached their games' highlights distinctively by making them longer, like with the Italy vs England final with a 25min video (1,517s).

Still on the video length, as can be seen in Table A.2, the statistically significant correlations found across the channels was that longer videos had more views, likes and comments – whilst for SuperSport (South Africa), the only statistically significant correlation was with comments. As such, whilst some shorter videos were clearly outliers in terms of views, as we could see in Figure A.1 – especially with a meme video with Cristiano Ronaldo (Portuguese player) and Paul Pogba (French player) on Optus Sport that had over 7 million views – what the data indicates is that users are approaching YouTube as a potential substitute to the traditional medium of TV and *expecting* videos that possess similar characteristics in terms of production, length and content. Therefore, whilst in media circles it is commonly argued that social media platforms instil a culture of immediacy by reinforcing a perceived *shorter attention span*, what the data showed across the channels was that the longer the video, more views and active engagements such as likes and comments happened. Whilst based on the data we have access to via the API it is impossible to categorically affirm with a degree of certainty that users are watching the entire video, we can use active engagement as a proxy for it and deduce that when users comment or like a video, it means that they have watched it in its *entire* duration, or at least a substantial amount of it.

Whilst active engagement can serve as a proxy for deducing the type of video in terms of duration that gets more attention, it can also provide further evidence of how YouTube is being used by content creators and their audiences. As mentioned earlier, YouTube acts as a potential substitute to the more traditional medium of TV because of the content that is shared by complementors, but also because of the way audiences consume on the platform. If we look at the active/passive ratio across all channels the data is somehow consistent with more passive cultural consumption practices, akin to the one performed on TV. As seen in Table A.1, the active/passive ratio varied between 0.025 to 0.008, with ITV being a clear outlier as they disabled the comment function on all their videos. Notably, this *low* active/passive ratio means that, even though YouTube has technological affordances that allow for more user engagement through commenting and liking, users are still consuming primarily through watching and replicating what they commonly do upon watching TV. Whilst the channels were statistically different between them when running non-parametric tests (see Kruskall-Wallis' results Table A.3 and representations on Figures A.2 to A.6), there were still some channels sharing similar approaches in their content remediation, and subsequently audiences' use such, as the following pairs in terms of active/passive (see Table A.4).

In sum, whilst YouTube currently provides a further space for mediating – and particularly remediating – the spectacle of the Euros and attaching additional layers to the experience of consuming the Euros to a point where immediacies are generated for audiences across the world, it is still very much an alternative to the primary medium of TV. Whilst the most-viewed video across all channels – Pogba and Ronaldo's meme on Optus Sport – amassed over 7 million views and the following 4 in the top 5 had on average 3 million views – highlights of Switzerland v France (ESPN FC USA), Italy v England (tvN Sport), Italy v England (ESPN FC USA), and Portugal v France (TUDN Mexico) – those figures are substantially lower than live audiences on TV (for a comparison, see ESPN Newsroom, 2021). Despite this, because of the YouTube-sport nexus's infancy in comparison to the long-established relationship between TV and live football broadcasting, it is possible to expect that not only consumption will become more active on YouTube, but that those more active practices will have a long-lasting influence on how audiences hope content is created for TV.

Conclusion

This chapter elucidates the argument that YouTube constitutes another dynamic layer in the global remediation of the Euros. As products of their times (Roche, 2017), sport mega-events are no longer solely produced or consumed through television, print media or radio. Rather, the 'media event' facet of mega-events that scholars observed (Bourdieu, 1998; Billings, 2008; Rowe, 1996) has been reconfigured by the emergence of new digital technologies and social media platforms. These provide new ways through which broadcasters can connect with their audiences. Hence, this chapter built on Chapter 3 and showcased how YouTube, in the case of Euro 2020, was employed by broadcasters to remediate and repurpose the live football game experience. By analysing 17 rights holders of Euro 2020 located *in* and *beyond* Europe, this chapter's arguments are that YouTube overall (1) reinforced this mega-event's global reach and that (2) the remediation that occurs on the platform symbolizes an alternative to television, which is approached by users as providing a substitutive cultural football consumption experience.

Such an argument is particularly important because it demonstrates that YouTube – whilst unable to outright replace the traditional televised experience of the mega-events (Tang and Cooper, 2018) – transforms and adds new dynamics to the mega-event experience (see Lee Ludvigsen and Petersen-Wagner, 2022). The broadcasters' adaptions to YouTube thus play a central role in the transformation of global audiences' cultural consumption practices, as these audiences become increasingly (inter-)active. In a way, this touches the surface of the fluid relationship between sport, television and media which is constantly shaped by global forces (Rowe, 1996). Hence, as this chapter adds to the limited literature on the European Championships on social media, it can be asserted that YouTube remains one key source for the content and global coverage associated with this mega-event.

Note

1 We collected metrics from the following channels' Euro 2020 playlists: BBC Sport and ITV Sport (UK); beIN Sports (France); ESPN FC (USA); Magenta

Sport (Germany); NOS Sport (Netherlands); Rai (Italy); TUDN (Mexico); Sporza and RTBFSport (Belgium); SRF Sport (Switzerland); Optus Sport (Australia); TNT Sports (Argentina); TSN (Canada); SuperSport (South Africa); tvN Sports (South Korea); Stadium Astro (Malaysia).

References

Alphabet (2022) *Q4 & Fiscal Year*. Available at: https://abc.xyz/investor/static/pdf/20220202_alphabet_10K.pdf?cache=fc81690 (accessed 25/07/2022).

Apple (2022) *Apple and Major League Soccer to Present all MLS Matches Around the World for 10 Years, Beginning in 2023*. Available at: www.apple.com/uk/newsroom/2022/06/apple-and-mls-to-present-all-mls-matches-for-10-years-beginning-in-2023/ (accessed 25/07/2022).

Bärtl M (2018) YouTube channels, uploads and views: A statistical analysis of the past 10 years. *Convergence: The International Journal of Research into New Media Technologies* 24(1): 16–32.

Billings A (2008) *Olympic Media: Inside the Biggest Show on Television*. London: Routledge.

Bolter JD and Grusin R (2000) *Remediation: Understanding New Media*. Cambridge, MA: MIT Press.

Bourdieu P (1998) *On Television*. New York: New York Press.

Briggs A and Burke P (2020) *A Social History of the Media: From Gutenberg to Facebook*. Cambridge: Polity Press.

Buraimo B, Simmons R and Szymanski S (2006) English football. *Journal of Sport Economics* 7(1): 29–46.

Burgess J and Green J (2018) *YouTube: Online Video and Participatory Culture*. Cambridge: Polity.

Checchinato F, Disegna M and Gazzola P (2015) Content and feedback analysis of YouTube videos: Football clubs and fans as brand communities. *Journal of Creative Communications* 10(1): 71–88.

Chisari F (2006) When football went global: Televising the 1966 World Cup. *Historical Social Research* 31(1): 42–54.

Dart J (2014) New media, professional sport and political economy. *Journal of Sport & Social Issues* 38(6): 528–547.

Dayan D and Katz E (1992) *Media Events: The Live Broadcasting of History*. Cambridge, MA: Harvard University Press.

Debord G (1999) *The Society of Spectacle*. New York: Zone Books.

ESPN Newsroom (2021) *UEFA EURO 2020 Final on ESPN is the Most-Viewed Euro Match Ever in the U.S. with 6,488,000 Viewers*. Available at: https://espnpressroom.com/us/press-releases/2021/07/uefa-euro-2020-final-on-espn-is-the-most-viewed-euro-match-ever-in-the-u-s-with-6488000-viewers/ (accessed 10/08/2022).

FIFA (2018) *The 2018 FIFA World Cup in Numbers*. Available at: https://digitalhub.fifa.com/m/30671157c4e089f3/original/veij99mubas9idvf47rl-pdf.pdf (accessed 12/11/2021).

Galily Y (2014) When the medium becomes 'well done': Sport, television, and technology in the twenty-first century. *Television & New Media* 15(8): 717–724.

Galily Y and Tamir I (2014) A match made in heaven?! Sport, television, and new media in the beginning of the third millennia. *Television & New Media* 15(8): 699–702.

Gantz W and Lewis N (2014) Sports on traditional and newer digital media. *Television & New Media* 15(8): 760–768.

Garcia B, Niemann A and Grant W (2011) Conclusion. In: A Niemann, B Garcia and W Grant (eds.) *The Transformation of European Football: Towards the Europeanisation of the National Game*. Manchester: Manchester University Press.

The Guardian (2016) *Champions League and Europa League Finals Attract 3m YouTube Viewers for BT*. Available at: www.theguardian.com/media/2016/may/31/champions-league-and-europa-league-finals-attract-3m-youtube-viewers-for-bt (accessed 25/07/2022).

The Guardian (2021) *Premier League Renews £4.8bn TV Deal with Extra £100m Trickle-down Funds*. Available at: www.theguardian.com/football/2021/may/12/premier-league-set-for-45bn-new-tv-deal-with-sky-bt-and-amazon (accessed 25/07/2022).

The Guardian (2022) *Amazon Close to Deal Over Champions League Rights in UK*. Available at: www.theguardian.com/business/2022/jun/30/amazon-close-to-secure-deal-over-champions-league-rights-in-uk (accessed 25/07/2022).

Hutchins B and Rowe D (2009) From broadcast scarcity to digital plenitude. *Television & New Media* 10(4): 354–370.

Hutchins B and Rowe D (2012) *Sport beyond Television: The Internet, Digital Media and the Rise of Networked Media Sport*. London: Routledge.

Jarret K (2008) Beyond broadcast yourself™: The future of YouTube. *Media International Australia* 126(1): 132–144.

Jenkins H (2006) *Convergence Culture: Where Old and New Media Collide*. New York: New York University Press.

Lee Ludvigsen JA and Petersen-Wagner R (2022) From television to YouTube: Digitalised sport mega-events in the platform society. *Leisure Studies*: 1–18.

Lobato R (2016) The cultural logic of digital intermediaries: YouTube multichannel networks. *Convergence: The International Journal of Research into New Media Technologies* 22(4): 348–360.

Lobato R and Meese J (2016) *Geoblocking and Global Video Culture*. Amsterdam: Institute of Network Cultures.

Marivoet S (2006) UEFA Euro 2004™ Portugal: The social construction of a sports mega-event and spectacle. *The Sociological Review* 54(2): 127–143.

McCarthy B (2021) Reinvention through CrossFit: Branded transformation documentaries. *Communication & Sport* 9(1): 150–165.

McQuail D and Deuze M (2020) *McQuail's Media and Mass Communication Theory*. London: SAGE.

Meese J and Podkalicka A (2016) Circumvention, media sport and the fragmentation of video culture. In: R Lobato and J Meese (eds.) *Geoblocking and Global Video Culture*. Amsterdam: Institute of Network Cultures, pp. 74–85.

Newman M (2010) New media, young audiences and discourses of attention: From Seasame Street to 'snack culture'. *Media, Culture & Society* 32(4): 581–596.

Ørmen J and Gregersen A (2022) Towards the engagement economy: Interconnected processes of commodification on YouTube. *Media, Culture & Society* OnlineFirst: 1–21.

Petersen-Wagner R (2018) Between old and new traditions: Transnational solidarities and the love for Liverpool FC. In: S Lawrence and G Crawford (eds.) *Digital Football Cultures: Fandom, Identities and Resistance*. London: Routledge.

Petersen-Wagner R (2022) The business of FIFA World Cup: Digital and social media. In: S Chadwick, D Parnell, P Widdop and C Anagnostopoulos (eds.) *The Business of FIFA World Cup*. London: Routledge.

Petersen-Wagner R and Lee Ludvigsen JA (2022a) The Video Assistant Referee (VAR) as neo-coloniality of power? Fan negative reactions to VAR in the 2018 FIFA Men's World Cup. *Sport in Society*: 1–15.

Petersen-Wagner R and Lee Ludvigsen JA (2022b) Digital transformations in a platform society: A comparative analysis of European football leagues as YouTube complementors. *Convergence: The International Journal of Research into New Media Technologies*: 1–22.

Poell T, Nieborg D and Duffy BE (2022) *Platforms and Cultural Production*. Cambridge: Polity Press.

Rivers D and Ross A (2021) 'This channel has more subs from rival fans than Arsenal fans': Arsenal Fan TV, football fandom and banter in the new media era. *Sport in Society* 24(6): 867–885.

Roche M (2017) *Mega-Events and Social Change: Spectacle, Legacy and Public Culture*. Manchester: Manchester University Press.

Rowe D (1996) The global love-match: Sport and television. *Media, Culture & Society* 18(4): 565–582.

Rowe D (2004) *Sport, Culture and the Media: The Unruly Trinity*. Maidenhead: Open University Press.

Sandvoss C (2003) *A Game of Two Halves: Football, Television and Globalization*. London: Routledge.

Statista (2021) *Main news Sources Used by Gen Z or Millennials vs. Total Consumers Worldwide as of February 2021*. Available at: www.statista.com/statistics/281915/main-news-sources-millennials/ (accessed 13/04/2022).

Statista (2022a) *Most Popular Platforms for Daily News Consumption in the United States as of February 2022, by Age Group*. Available at: www.statista.com/statistics/717651/most-popular-news-platforms/ (accessed 11/07/2022).

Statista (2022b) *TV Ratings of the Super Bowl in the United States from 1990 to 2022*. Available at: www.statista.com/statistics/216538/super-bowl-us-tv-ratings/ (accessed 11/07/2022).

Statista (2022c) *Most Popular Social Networks Worldwide as of January 2022, Ranked by Number of Monthly Active Users*. Available at: www.statista.com/statistics/272014/global-social-networks-ranked-by-number-of-users/ (accessed 25/07/2022).

Stauff M (2009) Sports on YouTube. In: P Snickars and P Vonderau (eds.) *The YouTube Reader*. Stockholm: National Library of Sweden, pp. 236–251.

Tang T and Cooper R (2018) The most social games: Predictors of social media uses during the 2016 Rio Olympics. *Communication & Sport* 6(3): 308–330.

Thorburn D and Jenkins H (2004) *Rethinking Media Change: The Aesthetics of Transition.* Cambridge, MA: MIT Press.

UEFA (2021a) *Where to Watch the UEFA Euro 2020 Final: TV Broadcast Partners, Live Streams.* Available at: www.uefa.com/uefaeuro/history/news/025a-0ec0d02154c8-5fa71e862f15-1000-where-to-watch-euro-2020/ (accessed 01/06/2022).

UEFA (2021b) *UEFA Euro 2020 Impresses with 5.2 Billion Cumulative Global Live Audience.* Available at: www.uefa.com/insideuefa/about-uefa/news/026d-132519672495-56a014558e80-1000-uefa-euro-2020-impresses-with-5-2-billion-cumulative-global-liv/ (accessed 08/07/2022).

Whannel G (1985) Television spectacle and the Internationalization of sport. *Journal of Communication Inquiry* 9(2): 54–74.

Whannel G (1986) The unholy alliance: Notes on television and the remaking of British sport 1965–85. *Leisure Sciences* 5(2): 129–145.

Whannel G (1992) *Fields in Vision: Television Sport and Cultural Transformation.* London: Routledge.

World Bank (2022) *Population, Total – European Union.* Available at: https://data.worldbank.org/indicator/SP.POP.TOTL?locations=EU (accessed 08/07/2022).

YouTube (2022a) *YouTube for Press.* Available at: https://blog.youtube/press/ (accessed 07/04/2022).

YouTube (2022b) *Upload Videos Longer than 15 Minutes.* Available at: https://support.google.com/youtube/answer/71673?co=GENIE.Platform%3DAndroid&hl=en (accessed 15/02/2022).

YouTube (2022c) *YouTube Live Streaming & Premieres.* Available at: www.youtube.com/intl/ALL_uk/howyoutubeworks/product-features/live/ (accessed 25/07/2022).

YouTube (2022d) *Get Started with YouTube Shorts.* Available at: https://support.google.com/youtube/answer/10059070?hl=en-GB (accessed 25/07/2022).

5 The politics of co-bidding and hosting

Nordic alliances and football's 'coming home' (again)?

Introduction

This chapter investigates the politics of mega-event co-bidding and co-hosting. Rowe (2012: 287) reminds us that: 'Although mega-events are intermittent, the process of seeking to host them, and of adjudicating between competing bids, is continuous'. It is also a process that has evolved over the last three decades as this chapter demonstrates, focusing on the processes associated with joint bidding and hosting in the Euros' context. In Chapter 2, we first highlighted how sport mega-events have become increasingly complex projects and, second, how events activate certain interest-driven interactions between sport's governing bodies and nation-states. For example, it is normal practice that host countries (or cities) are required to guarantee that they will allocate funds towards and meet the requirements, criterion and standards set out by the governing body owning the relevant event's rights.

Further, in the present day, mega-events have been criticized by several commentators, social movements and academics because of their financial and social costs (Talbot, 2021). This connects to mega-events' position as risky undertakings for host nations, cities and governments (Flyvbjerg et al., 2021; Lee Ludvigsen, 2022a). Indeed, Müller (2015) even presents that it is possible to speak of what he calls the 'mega-event syndrome': a diagnosis capturing the complex financial, urban, legal and bidding-related issues that tend to pop up around many contemporary mega-events. Against this backdrop some countries have, historically and recently, faced backlash in their pursuit of hosting rights, and mega-event hosting has become increasingly contentious. This has in part been demonstrated by a rise in bid withdrawals or uninterested candidates (Byun et al., 2019; Lauermann, 2022).

Importantly, under these conditions, it is observable that the formation of international joint event bids has become increasingly common in the mega-event world (Beissel and Kohe, 2020; Byun et al., 2019). This can be defined as the event bids where 'two or more countries [are] coming

DOI: 10.4324/9781003359098-5

together under a cobranded identity to form a proactive strategic partnership in an effort to gain the right to host a sport event' (Byun et al., 2021: 354). However, this also symbolizes a break away from the standard format where *one* country typically has pursued an event's hosting rights as the sole host/bidder (Lee Ludvigsen, 2019). As the timeline of European Championships post-2000 revealed (Chapter 2), such bids have – in some cases – been successful, and the editions of the Euros have consequently been hosted by more than one country.

In fact, the trends of co-bidding and co-hosting are specifically prominent in the Euros' context. Since 2000, four European Championships have been staged by more than one country (in 2000, 2008, 2012 and 2020) compared to one FIFA World Cup (2002).[1] Concurrently, a number of unsuccessful joint bids or bid alliances have materialized too, although these have generated little scholarly discussion. Thus, by connecting with the growing literature on sport mega-event co-bidding and hosting (Byun et al., 2019, 2021; Wise and Lee Ludvigsen, 2022; Beissel and Kohe, 2020), this chapter examines alliances set up in the Nordic region aiming to secure the European Championships and discusses the prospects and politics of the anticipated joint UK and Irish bid for Euro 2028. As we argue, co-hosting and bidding practices remain important to examine – whether the relevant bids turn out successful or not – because they reveal more general developments in the political fields of mega-events. Such developments include aspirations of political cooperation and social legacies, but also issues such as lack of political support and concerns about delivery costs in a time where some nations and politicians seem increasingly aware of what we unpack next: the 'mega-event syndrome' (Müller, 2015).

Conceptualization: event bidding, pitfalls and the 'mega-event syndrome'

The bidding process for sport mega-events stretches over several years. Although an event's hosting rights are commonly considered as highly regarded and prestigious, some countries, as discussed here, have abstained from entering the hosting rights bidding stages in recent years. As Parent (2013) points out, the bidding for a sporting event is a process that can take between 1 to 3 years, and it consists of separate stages: for example, gaining support, financing, planning and logistical and infrastructural considerations, before the candidate(s) submit a bid document to the event owner. In itself, the bidding process thus involves an array of stakeholders including states, cities, politicians and national sports federations. Indeed, the current status and complexity of event bidding is also partly illustrated by the emergence of so-called 'bid professionals' who carry out consultancy work that assists nations or cities with the creation of visions or rationales for their bids (Horne and Takahashi, 2022). As such, every formulated mega-event bid possesses unique characteristics and although the submitted bid may not be successful, each bid still represents an assemblage of visions speaking to the future of a specific city or country and configures networks of individuals and organizations that could be reactivated in other sporting-related contexts.

Concerning why countries seek to bid for an event, the literature point towards various motivations and visions. As already noted, some countries seek to acquire hosting rights and use events as catalysts for a positive 'legacy', such as enhanced sport participation, an economic boost (Parent, 2013) or for a more myopic 'feel-good' high across the population (Black, 2007). Concurrently, it is also clear that mega-event staging is closely tied to the arena of global politics. Therefore, some countries, attracted by mega-events' global exposure, have sought to use them as moments to demonstrate their economic and technological capabilities to improve 'external perceptions of a country' (Grix, 2012: 7) and legitimacy on the international scene (Brannagan and Rookwood, 2016). Recent years have also seen a growth in research investigating the role of mega-events in states' soft power strategies (Grix et al., 2015; Brannagan and Rookwood, 2016).

As central to this book, mega-events like the European Championships are strongly intertwined with political strategies, actors and circumstances. Already from the Euros' bidding stage, interactions and negotiations are ongoing between states, football federations and UEFA, which revolve around event-specific requirements, standards and the mentioned guarantees that aspiring host nations must provide to UEFA (Włoch, 2013). Broadly, however, as the financial costs, complexity and size of mega-events have consistently increased (Chapter 2), one may observe that some countries, cities and their governments have become increasingly aware of the pitfalls that are associated with submitting – and possibly even winning – mega-event hosting rights (Lauermann, 2022). Such a stance has also been fuelled by concerns about mega-events' impacts on human rights and the environment, as well as the special requirements that host countries have to accommodate (Tangen, 2022), including stadium specifications, VIP amenities, tax concessions and urban infrastructural transformations (Kennedy, 2017). In sum, this – coupled with post-event stories of so-called 'white elephants' (Lee Ludvigsen, 2021, 2022a), cost overruns and schedule delays – has meant that there seems to be a greater general awareness of what can be called the 'mega-event syndrome' (Müller, 2015).

Although he focuses primarily on the FIFA World Cup and the Olympics, Müller (2015) first introduced the term 'mega-event syndrome' to explain the pitfalls of mega-events and why obstacles and challenges so commonly come to characterize the planning for mega-events. Following Müller, there are seven symptoms of the mega-event syndrome, including: (1) overpromising of benefits, (2) underestimation of costs, (3) event take-over, (4) public risk taking, (5) rule of exception, (6) elite capture and (7) event fix. Whereas each symptom, due to space restrictions, will not be broken down in detail here, the consequences of these symptoms speak broadly to a range of financial, social and urban impacts, including misallocation of resources, oversized infrastructure and loss of public trust.

Whilst Müller provides a range of different radical and less radical changes that could be enabled to address the symptoms of the mega-event syndrome, one of the changes he proposes relates to the potential *decentralization* of mega-events. Although he does not seem to refer specifically to co-hosting here, he argues that: 'It makes more sense to spread demand spatially rather than build permanent facilities to accommodate peak demand' (ibid.: 14). Compared to the Olympics, however, football mega-events are typically more decentralized, and its fixtures are allocated to different cities spread across a host country. Yet it could be suggested that one way to address the mega-event syndrome, situated within and co-existing with Müller's proposed solution of decentralization, is the co-hosting of events, especially when the relevant events rely on already-built – rather than completely new – stadiums (Lee Ludvigsen, 2019). Here, the European Championships has been pioneering through its employment of co-hosts and UEFA's evaluations of joint bids.

Sharing the Euros: strategic alliances and the politics of co-hosting

Whilst the European Championships have not received the same levels of criticism for the event's associated financial costs or grandiose requirements as the FIFA World Cup or the Olympics, the level of planning, stadium and transport requirements and agreed timelines associated with the Euros still remain highly complex and have, as discussed later, contributed to some countries withdrawing their candidacy for their hosting rights. Indeed, some of the symptoms of the mega-event syndrome are undoubtedly identifiable in the context of contemporary championships – even in cases of co-hosting – including the rule of exception (see Chapter 6 on Euro 2016) and overpromising of benefits (for a discussion on Ukraine in 2012, see *The Guardian*, 2013). Furthermore, it remains pertinent here to return to the tournament's gradual expansion of teams which in turn has generated a greater need for high-capacity stadiums and state-of-the-art infrastructures.

However, when compared to the Olympic Games and the World Cup, the Euros – or UEFA specifically – has been pioneering in its employment of co-hosts. After the Netherlands and Belgium's successful Euro 2000 – which was the first mega-event hosted by more than one country – it is evident how other UEFA-countries have launched joined bids for upcoming European Championships. Similarly, we may also observe that this trend has spread beyond Europe and beyond football. In 2026, Mexico, Canada and the US will co-host the FIFA men's World Cup (Beissel and Kohe, 2020), and in 2023 New Zealand and Australia will join forces to stage the FIFA women's World Cup (Beissel et al., 2022). Joint bids are also evident in sports such as handball and basketball (Byun et al., 2021).

Following the Dutch/Belgian Euro 2000, five joint bids entered the competition for Euro 2008's hosting rights. Whereas the alliance of Austria and Switzerland won the rights to this tournament in 2002, it had to compete with joint bids from Bosnia-Herzegovina/Croatia, Denmark/Finland/Norway/Sweden, Greece/Turkey and Scotland/Ireland. A few years later, when Ukraine and Poland successfully acquired the rights to host Euro 2012, this alliance had faced a rivalling bid by Croatia and Hungary (Byun et al., 2021). Arguably, the bidding stage of the European Championships over the last 30 years has been characterized by the rise of bidding alliances

This raises the question of *why* more countries have joined forces to launch joint bids. To address this, Byun et al. (2019) highlight that this trend is explained partially by the potentially reduced costs inflicted upon hosts who share an event's hosting rights. Moreover, it can also increase the public appeal for bids, whilst allowing bidders to share tangible and intangible resources in the form of stadiums, pre-existing knowledge and event housing experience, which can boost the eventual application. Hence, in a response to the increasingly multifaceted and competitive processes of event bidding – and the existing risks arriving *with* hosting rights – it can be argued that the 'formation of joint bids has been used as a strategy to gain competitive advantage' (Byun et al., 2021: 559). Not only do joint bids potentially reduce the number of rivalling bidders, but as Byun et al. (2019, 2021) argue, joint bids can be understood as *strategic alliances* which rely on collaborative efforts and resource sharing between the alliance's partners in order to achieve a specific aim (winning hosting rights). Notwithstanding, they also note that in spite of the 'increase in joint bids there has been a lack of attention given to the topic within academia' (Byun et al., 2019: 53).

One particularly important aspect of joint bids in the context of the Euros relates to their wider 'pan-European' connections, as mentioned in Chapter 1. Whereas co-hosting indeed may provide keen hosts – who are geographically close – the possibility of sharing resources, responsibilities and infrastructures, joint bids also carry a deeper political significance. Thus far, in the cases of the co-hosted European Championships, the tournaments of 2000, 2008 and 2012 reveal that the co-host countries have shared a geographic border. Yet, it is also worth noticing how Euro 2008 and Euro 2012 were hosted by *one* EU country and *one* non-EU country.

With regards to event bidding, Włoch (2013) highlights that Ukraine and Poland, in their shared bid, emphasized how a shared Euro 2012 would promote the countries' integration into Europe. Indeed, in Poland, Euro 2012 was compared with the country's membership in the EU and NATO and discourses highlighted how Euro 2012 could be a catalyst for processes of Europeanization and modernization within the country (see Jaskulowski and Surmiak, 2016). In a way, it could be argued that the awarding of hosting rights to co-hosts that are EU and non-EU members presents one tool through which UEFA drives forward or at least contributes to ideas of a 'shared' Europe (Chapter 1).

The use of non-EU and EU hosts may also bring about complications. In the case of Euro 2008, Klauser (2011) posits that Switzerland's position as a non-EU country had certain organizational and security-related implications for the tournament. As Klauser writes, before 2008 Switzerland had not yet implemented the EU Schengen Agreement on European police cooperation. Furthermore, temporary special arrangement with regards to border controls had to be made ahead of the tournament for border security purposes. Most recently, Euro 2020 also took place across a mixture of EU and non-EU countries, with non-EU countries such as Russia, the UK and Azerbaijan staging fixtures. At the same time, the multi-country Euro 2020 represented a one-off occasion that UEFA is unlikely to replicate in the future due to cited issues of long travelling distances between EU and non-EU countries, and challenges related to different jurisdictions (Lee Ludvigsen, 2022b).

This illustrates how joint bids and co-hosting are not merely results of geographic realities. Joint bids and co-hosting are highly politicized undertakings that have specific visions about the specific countries, regions or Europe ingrained within them. On the one hand, they can (if successful) act as tools through which European collaboration or integration – beyond EU level – is enacted by event's distinct hosting visions and characteristics. On the other hand, co-hosted events may also serve as expressions of the challenges of European integration (e.g., the changes to the Schengen Agreement). Whilst earlier work on co-hosted Euros (Włoch, 2013; Klauser, 2011; Lee Ludvigsen, 2021; Jaskulowski and Surmiak, 2016) provides us with an understanding of the cultural politics of these events, we know far less about those bids that have remained unsuccessful or that are under construction. The next subsections therefore discuss the failed Nordic attempts to gain the hosting rights for the Euros, and the prospects of a UK/Irish Euro 2028 bid.

Nordic hosting aspirations

One of the unsuccessful bid alliances that entered the competition for the Euro 2008 hosting rights was formed by Denmark, Finland, Norway and Sweden (Byun et al., 2021). Yet, apart from brief mentions in the existing literature, there are few – if any – accounts of this failed bid and the other Nordic attempts to host the Euros after 2000. In this sense, this section examines one failed and one withdrawn bid for the European Championships originating from the Nordic region and we place these in context of wider trends speaking to mega-event withdrawals in Norway and Sweden.

The Nordic region has proud and longstanding traditions of mega-event hosting. For example, in the twentieth century, Norway and Sweden staged the 1912 Summer Olympics (Sweden), the 1958 and 1994 Winter Olympics (Norway) and the 1992 Euros (Sweden) (Pujik, 2000; Yttergren and Bolling, 2012). More recently, Denmark's *Parken Stadium* (Copenhagen) hosted four Euro 2020 fixtures. Notwithstanding these, recent developments indicate an increased reluctance towards the pursuit of hosting rights in the Nordic region, especially in Norway and Sweden. Whilst the capital cities Oslo and Stockholm separately considered submitting applications for the 2022 Winter Olympics, the two capitals never proceeded with their final applications to the International Olympic Committee (IOC). This was mostly because the two governments perceived a committed bid to be a risky endeavour (see Paulsson and Alm, 2020). In the years prior to this, the Norwegian city Tromsø had also been considered a candidate for a bid for the Winter Olympics in 2014 and 2018 (Seippel et al., 2016), although this also never materialized. However, in the football world, we may see the convergence of Nordic bid alliances, although these have been unsuccessful or been withdrawn.

The mentioned Nordic 2008 bid was announced in 2001. This bid was promoted under the banner of 'When the Saga Comes True' and designed to take place across two already-built stadiums in all the involved countries, which included Denmark, Finland, Sweden and Norway (BBC, 2002), in order to accommodate UEFA's requirements speaking to eight stadiums (Byun et al., 2019). A year later, the bid was presented at a UEFA event for bid presentations in Nyon, Switzerland, in June 2002 (UEFA, 2002). Yet, six months later, the dream of a 'pan-Nordic' Euros was crushed as the bid ended fourth when Austria and Switzerland won the majority of votes and Euro 2008's hosting rights. The defeat, however, did not symbolize the end of Norway and Sweden's aspirations to host the Euros.

It is suggested that 'if bidders have been involved in alliances before they are more likely to form joint bids' (Byun et al., 2019: 47). Reinforcing this,

Norway and Sweden – following the failed Nordic 2008 bid – continued to work together, and in 2009 the countries announced that they had begun the work for a joint Euro 2016 bid. This preparatory work involved the selection of stadiums and host cities and plans for new national arenas in the two countries. In a joint statement from the two football federations, it was reported that: 'We are cooperating really well and have done extensive preparation work' (quoted in World Soccer, 2009).

However, despite the extensive preparation work, this planned bid was never presented or submitted to UEFA. Whilst UEFA had announced their decision to expand from 16 to 24 qualified teams ahead of Euro 2016 – hence reconfiguring the requirements speaking to stadiums and infrastructure (Chapter 2) – the reasoning behind the abandoned 2016 bid must also be understood in light of the high financial costs and lack of guarantees that the two relevant governments were willing to provide to the national football federations.

During the planning stages, the Norwegian newspaper *Verdens Gang* (2009) reported that a pre-bid report was commissioned to explore the feasibility of a Norwegian and Swedish bid. Importantly, the conclusions of this report became a turning point for the aspiring bidders. The report, worked out by two private consultancy firms, concluded that the Norwegian-Swedish bid appeared unrealistic in its scope and would come at enormous cost. Figures that were reported maintained that in Norway, the event could end up costing up to 6.4 billion NOK (NRK, 2009). Seemingly, the flurry of high costs, limited political support and the expanding tournament format must be seen as contributing towards the withdrawal of the Norwegian-Swedish bid. Hence, by the time the deadline for submitting a bid for Euro 2016 had expired, Italy, France and Turkey were the three candidates who submitted a bid to UEFA's executive committee (UEFA, 2010a). Ultimately, the hosting rights were won by France, who received seven votes to Turkey's six (UEFA, 2010b).

Whilst the Nordic 2008 bid and Norway and Sweden's planned Euro 2016 bid failed and was withdrawn respectively, they still remain relevant for the study of mega-events because they demonstrate how there have been significant attempts within the Nordic region to enter alliances for the purpose of the European Championships since the turn of the millennium. Significantly, the lack of political support for Sweden and Norway's joint Euro 2016 bid in distinct ways mirrors the stories of the two countries' separate 2022 Winter Olympics bids that, similarly, were never submitted. In these cases, too, the risk of financial deficits and lack of governmental financial guarantees emerged as two of the key obstacles for launched bids (see Paulsson and Alm, 2020).

However, whereas Nordic countries are yet to stage any of the largest global football events in tandem, they have done so in other sports. Sweden and Norway (and Austria) hosted the 2020 European Championships in handball and an alliance of Denmark, Norway and Sweden were recently awarded the rights to host the same tournament for men (in 2026) and women (in 2028) under the banner of 'Scandinavian Connect' (Norwegian Handball Federation, 2021), suggesting that bid alliances compose an important part of the Nordic countries' sport policies and repertoires *vis-a-vis* sporting events.

Taken together, the examples discussed here therefore illustrate, first, the emergence of strategic alliances across the Nordic region *vis-a-vis* football mega-events. Possibly, they suggest that even failed or withdrawn bids can formulate 'legacies' in the form of alliances, relationships or networks that could be reactivated or re-oriented towards new events. For example, Denmark, Sweden and Norway – together with the Faroe Islands, Iceland and Finland – expressed an interest in the hosting rights for Euro 2024 and 2028, although a bid never emerged (Reuters, 2016). Though as shown, alliances in themselves do not automatically translate into *submitted* bids. Second, the withdrawn Euro 2016 bid also shows that even in cases of joint bids, some of the symptoms of the mega-event syndrome (cf. Müller, 2015), especially those speaking to financial costs, may deter potential host countries and erode the necessary political support.

Uniting for 2028: football's 'coming home' (again)?

At the time of writing, the bidding process for Euro 2028 is underway. One of the likely bids that has been discussed in the media and political quarters is a joint bid between the UK and Ireland. As UEFA (2022) confirmed, this bid will compete with Turkey, as Russia – who had declared an interest – had their bid dismissed following the Russian-led invasion of Ukraine in February 2022 (Sky Sports, 2022).

Initially, the football associations of England, Northern Ireland, Scotland, Wales and Ireland had formed an alliance to work towards a bid for another mega-event: the 2030 FIFA World Cup. Yet in light of the findings in a conducted feasibility study, this project was abandoned so that the alliance could direct their sole focus on Euro 2028 (The FA, 2022). If successful, 2028 will not be the first time Ireland, Scotland and England co-host a European Championships, as they all were awarded Euro 2020 fixtures, even though Ireland was dropped a few months prior to the tournament's commencement due to the country's Covid-19 restrictions at the time (Lee Ludvigsen, 2022b).

As the English FA announced in February 2022, one of the main reasons for the bid alliance's focus on Euro 2028 – rather than the World Cup – related to the financial risk associated with the delivery costs. As their statement confirming their bid intention stated:

> Hosting a UEFA EURO offers a similar return on investment, with the European tournament carrying a *far lower delivery cost* and the potential of the benefits being realized sooner.
>
> (The FA, 2022, emphasis added)

Whilst the lower cost is referred to as important here, the joint bid has also been framed as potentially strengthening the relationship between the governments, whilst leaving positive impacts on host communities. As the Chief Executive of the English FA, Mark Bullingham, said:

> We think it's a brilliant opportunity for the five federations and governments to come together. . . . This is the third biggest sports event in the world and we've got a good opportunity to bring it to our collective countries and make a massively positive impact.
>
> (Quoted in *The Guardian*, 2022)

However, it should also be noted that the geopolitics of European football were cited as one of the reasons for the alliance's shift towards Euro 2028. With Spain and Portugal emerging as the favourite candidate from Europe for the 2030 World Cup bid, the CEO of the Irish FA, John Hill, commented that Euro 2028 appeared more 'winnable' than the World Cup because of: 'everything that has happened in relation to football geopolitics in the last six months' (quoted in the Daily Mail, 2022). Simultaneously, a country's mega-event ambitions do not necessarily correspond with those of local authorities or cities. In July 2022, reports emerged stating that numerous potential host cities in England 'could boycott' the Euro 2028 bid due to the associated terms and conditions and financial costs (*The Telegraph*, 2022).

Whereas the hosts of Euro 2028 and 2032 will be appointed in September 2023, there are already several aspects of the joint UK-Irish bid emerging that likely will have implications for both UK and European politics. First, should the bid be successful, Euro 2028 would represent another case of non-EU and EU countries sharing the hosting rights for an edition of the tournament, thereby opening up new questions of how the event might be framed in terms of 'Europe' given Ireland's status as an EU country and the UK's recent departure from the EU.

Second, and relatedly, concerning the UK, Euro 2028 would symbolize another 'post-Brexit' mega-event, succeeding Euro 2020, the 2022

Women's Euros and the 2022 Commonwealth Games. Thus, considering the UK's departure from the EU and its implications for its foreign policy and diplomacy (Dee and Smith, 2017), the UK's and specifically England's continual orientation toward mega-event hosting rights remains particularly interesting given the relationship between sporting events, soft power and foreign policy (Grix et al., 2015). In this line, sporting or cultural events may be utilized as platforms through which foreign publics' preferences are positively influenced by the exposure to a country's values, cultures or achievements (Woodward, 2020). With specific reference to the UK, the 2028 bid and the manifested ambition may hence represent an expression of how the country articulates a vision of itself to the wider world in this distinct period of transition.

Finally, the political *impact* that joint bids may represent remains relevant here. By understanding the UK as a political union (Keating, 2021) consisting of England, Northern Ireland, Scotland and Wales – who possess distinct constitutional and political identities (Anderson, 2021) and are all present in the 2028 bid – the pursuit of Euro 2028's hosting rights should also be considered to have a convergent frame attached to it. In the present day, 'post-Brexit' and 'post-Covid', where the union remains fractured and under pressure (Keating, 2021), a successful bid for (and a potentially well-organized) Euro 2028 could, in a way, serve as a sport-specific moment through which images of a momentum of collaborative working relationships across the union are conveyed, hence emphasizing the positive impact that co-hosting may be framed in terms of (Byun et al., 2021).

Conclusion

To conclude, the practices of co-bidding and co-hosting must be considered to involve highly politicized activities and, in terms of the wider mega-event milieu, two crucial trends. Significantly, mega-event bids are not merely constructed materially (in terms of stadiums, technical details, etc.) but socially, culturally and politically. Yet as Beissel et al. (2022: 772) highlight: 'there is a limited body of literature that examines ['joint mega-events'] strategic hosting visions, event legacies, and the geopolitical implications therein'. Against this backdrop, this chapter advances the scholarly discussion on co-hosting and bidding (Byun et al., 2019, 2021; Beissel and Kohe, 2020).

This chapter argues that joint bids and co-hosting must be considered key trends that have intensified in the same period wherein mega-events have been widely criticized for their gigantic financial costs, growing size and requirements (Müller, 2015). In such a context, countries' formations of bid alliances can enable them to share event costs, responsibilities, resources and stadium infrastructures and gain a competitive advantage (Byun et al., 2019). Moreover, co-hosting seems to have become increasingly attractive for host countries in accordance with the greater awareness of the pitfalls and the real and perceived risks that are associated with twenty-first century mega-events, which consequently has meant that 'hosting sport mega-events seems to have lost much of its glamour and appeal' in some parts of the world (Horne and Takahasi, 2022: 1). Whether co-hosting will become increasingly employed for the two largest sport mega-events (World Cup and the Olympics) remains to be seen. Undoubtedly, however, this remains a trend that is not solely of organizational or geographical relevance since it essentially has emerged intact with wider societal concerns (those of journalists, commentators, academics, civil society groups and politicians) about mega-events' socio-economic ramifications (Talbot, 2021).

As we maintain, the European Championships present a particularly illuminating arena for critically understanding the political dimensions that mark co-bidding and co-hosting. Whilst the Euros to date have been staged by more than one host on four occasions (in 2000, 2008, 2012 and 2021) and opened up joint ventures between non-EU and EU nations hosting tournaments, it is also important to pay attention to those bids that are under construction, unsuccessful or withdrawn because they can reveal wider sport mega-event developments. Notably, as the examples of the Nordic region and the joint British/Irish Euro 2028 bid illustrate, these alliances may fluctuate between different mega-events and also express visions of political cooperation, the concretized reluctance toward mega-events in some countries and the greater awareness of risks associated with mega-event hosting in the twenty-first century.

Note

1 Though the 2026 FIFA World Cup was awarded to three countries (USA, Canada and Mexico).

References

Anderson P (2021) The COVID-19 pandemic in the United Kingdom: A tale of convergence and divergence. In: N Steytler (eds.) *Comparative Federalism and COVID-19*. London: Routledge, pp. 142–159.

BBC (2002) *Euro 2008 Contenders*. Available at: http://news.bbc.co.uk/sport1/hi/football/2553465.stm (accessed 06/2022).

Beissel A and Kohe G (2020) United as one: The 2026 FIFA Men's World Cup hosting vision and the symbolic politics of legacy. *Managing Sport and Leisure*: 1–21.

Beissel A, Postlethwaite V and Grainger A (2022) 'Winning the women's World Cup': Gender, branding, and the Australia/New Zealand as one 2023 social media strategy for the FIFA Women's World Cup 2023™. *Sport in Society* 25(4): 768–798.

Black D (2007) The symbolic politics of sport mega-events: 2010 in comparative perspective. *Politikon* 34(3): 261–276.

Brannagan PM and Rookwood J (2016) Sports mega-events, soft power and soft disempowerment: International supporters' perspectives on Qatar's acquisition of the 2022 FIFA World Cup finals. *International Journal of Sport Policy and Politics* 8(2): 173–188.

Byun J, Ellis D and Leopkey B (2021) The pursuit of legitimacy through strategic alliances: The examination of international joint sport event bidding. *European Sport Management Quarterly* 21(4): 544–563.

Byun J, Leopkey B and Ellis D (2019) Understanding joint bids for international large-scale sport events as strategic alliances. *Sport, Business and Management: An International Journal* 10(1): 39–57.

Daily Mail (2022) *European Football 'Geopolitics' KO'd a UK and Ireland Bid for the 2030 World Cup.* Available at: www.dailymail.co.uk/sport/football/arti cle-10490781/European-football-geopolitics-KOd-UK-Ireland-bid-2030-World-Cup.html.

Dee D and Smith KE (2017) UK diplomacy at the UN after Brexit: Challenges and opportunities. *The British Journal of Politics and International Relations* 19(3): 527–542.

The FA (2022) *Five Associations Announce Joint Bid to Host UEFA EURO 2028 Across Five Countries.* Available at: www.thefa.com/news/2022/feb/07/state ment-uk-and-ireland-bid-for-euro-2028-20220702 (accessed 06/2022).

Flyvbjerg B, Budzier A and Lunn D (2021) Regression to the tail: Why the Olympics blow up. *Environment and Planning A: Economy and Space* 53(2): 233–260.

Grix J (2012) The politics of sports mega-events. *Political Insight* 3(1): 4–7.

Grix J, Brannagan PM and Houlihan B (2015) Interrogating states' soft power strategies: A case study of sports mega-events in Brazil and the UK. *Global Society* 29(3): 463–479.

The Guardian (2013) *Euro 2012 One Year on – Was It Worth It for Ukraine?* Available at: www.theguardian.com/football/blog/2013/jul/30/euro-2012-ukraine-one-year-on.

The Guardian (2022) *UK and Ireland to Launch Bid for Euro 2028 after Ditching World Cup Plans.* Available at: www.theguardian.com/football/2022/feb/07/ uk-and-ireland-to-launch-bid-for-euro-2028-after-ditching-world-cup-plans.

Horne J and Takahashi Y (2022) Mobile mega-event expertise in an 'East Asian era'. *Sociology of Sport Journal*: 1–10.

Jaskulowski K and Surmiak A (2016) Social construction of the impact of Euro 2012: A Wroclaw case study. *Leisure Studies* 35(5): 600–615.

Keating M (2021) *State and Nation in the United Kingdom: The Fractured Union.* Oxford: Oxford University Press.

Kennedy P (2017) Using Habermas to crack the European football championship. *Sport in Society* 20(3): 355–368.

Klauser F (2011) Commonalities and specificities in mega-event securitisation: The example of Euro 2008 in Austria and Switzerland. In: C Bennett and K Haggerty (eds.) *Security Games.* London: Routledge, pp. 120–136.

Lauermann J (2022) The declining appeal of mega-events in entrepreneurial cities: From Los Angeles 1984 to Los Angeles 2028. *Environment and Planning C: Politics and Space* 40(6): 1203–1218.

Lee Ludvigsen JA (2019) 'Continent-wide' sports spectacles: The 'multiple host format' of Euro 2020 and United 2026 and its implications. *Journal of Convention & Event Tourism* 20(2): 163–181.

Lee Ludvigsen JA (2021) Mega-events, expansion and prospects: Perceptions of Euro 2020 and its 12-country hosting format. *Journal of Consumer Culture*: 1–21.

Lee Ludvigsen JA (2022a) *Football and Risk: Trends and Perspectives*. London: Routledge.

Lee Ludvigsen JA (2022b) *Sport Mega-Events, Security and COVID-19: Securing the Football World*. London: Routledge.

Müller M (2015) The mega-event syndrome: Why so much goes wrong in mega-event planning and what to do about it. *Journal of the American Planning Association* 81(1): 6–17.

Norwegian Handball Federation (2021) *Norge, Sverige og Danmark Tildelt to EM*. Available at: www.handball.no/nyheter/2021/11/norge-sverige-og-danmark-til-delt-to-em/ (accessed 06/2022).

NRK (2009) *EM 2016: Sier nei til statsstøtte*. Available at: www.nrk.no/sport/fot-ball/em-2016_-sier-nei-til-statsstotte-1.6903298 (accessed 06/2022).

Parent M (2013) *Managing Major Sports Events* [1st edition]. London: Routledge.

Paulsson A and Alm J (2020) Passing on the torch: Urban governance, mega-event politics and failed Olympic bids in Oslo and Stockholm. *City, Culture and Society* 20: 1–11.

Puijk R (2000) A global media event? Coverage of the 1994 Lillehammer Olympic Games. *International Review for the Sociology of Sport* 35(3): 309–330.

Reuters (2016) *Nordic Countries to Make Joint Bid for Euro 2024, 2028*. Available at: www.reuters.com/article/uk-soccer-euros-nordics/nordic-countries-to-make-joint-bid-for-euro-2024-2028-idUKKCN0X00W8.

Rowe D (2012) The bid, the lead-up, the event and the legacy: Global cultural politics and hosting the Olympics. *The British Journal of Sociology* 63(2): 285–305.

Seippel Ø, Broch TB, Kristiansen E, Skille E, Wilhelmsen T, Strandbu Å and Thorjussen IM (2016) Political framing of sports: The mediated politicisation of Oslo's interest in bidding for the 2022 Winter Olympics. *International Journal of Sport Policy and Politics* 8(3): 439–453.

Sky Sports (2022) *Russia Disqualified from Women's Euros as Country's Bids for 2028 & 2032 Euros Deemed Ineligible by UEFA*. Available at: www.skysports.com/football/news/11095/12604207/russia-disqualified-from-womens-euros-as-countrys-bids-for-2028-2032-euros-deemed-ineligible-by-uefa#:~:text=Russia%20have%20been%20disqualified%20from,UEFA%20club%20competitions%20next%20season.

Talbot A (2021) Talking about the 'rotten fruits' of Rio 2016: Framing mega-event legacies. *International Review for the Sociology of Sport* 56(1): 20–35.

Tangen JO (2022) Observing the limits of steering-Norway's abortive Bid for the 2022 Olympic Winter Games in Oslo. *International Journal of Sport Policy and Politics* 14(1): 1–18.

The Telegraph (2022) *Debt-ridden Cities Could Boycott Euro 2028 bid After Being Asked to Foot Multi-million-Pound Bill.* Available at: www.telegraph.co.uk/football/2022/07/22/debt-ridden-cities-could-boycott-euro-2028-bid-asked-foot-multi/.

UEFA (2002) *EURO 2008 Bid Presentations.* Available at: www.uefa.com/insideuefa/about-uefa/news/0186-0f8-e2d8c22-56d8b0447372-1000--euro-2008-bid-presentations/.

UEFA (2010a) *UEFA European Football Championship Final Tournament 2016: Bid Evaluation Report.* Available at: www.uefa.com/MultimediaFiles/Download/MediaRelease/uefaorg/MediaReleases/01/48/83/27/1488327_DOWNLOAD.pdf (accessed 06/2022).

UEFA (2010b) *France to Host UEFA EURO 2016.* Available at: www.uefa.com/insideuefa/news/01e5-0f8-3881eb9-c3f172e6bb91-1000--france-to-host-uefa-uefaeuro2016/ (accessed 06/2022).

UEFA (2022) *Declarations of Interest in Hosting UEFA EURO 2028 and 2032 Received from Four Potential Bids.* Available at: www.uefa.com/insideuefa/mediaservices/mediareleases/news/0273-14b-3f7da5d-6b636cc7fc20-1000--declarations-of-interest-in-hosting-uefa-euro-2028-and-2032-rec/.

Verdens Gang (2009) *Kritisk Rapport om Norsk-Svensk EM-søknad.* Available at: www.vg.no/sport/fotball/i/8g4nW/kritisk-rapport-om-norsk-svensk-em-soeknad (accessed 06/2022).

Wise N and Lee Ludvigsen JA (2022) Uniting, disuniting and reuniting: Towards a 'United' 2026. *Sport in Society* 25(4): 837–846.

Włoch R (2013) UEFA as a new agent of Global Governance: A case study of relations between UEFA and the Polish Government against the background of the UEFA EURO 2012. *Journal of Sport and Social Issues* 37(3): 297–311.

Woodward R (2020) Sport and UK soft power: The case of Mount Everest. *The British Journal of Politics and International Relations* 22(2): 274–292.

World Soccer (2009) *Norway/Sweden Look at Joint Euro 2016 Bid.* Available at: www.worldsoccer.com/news/norwaysweden-look-at-joint-euro-2016-bid-277747 (accessed 06/2022).

Yttergren L and Bolling H (eds.) (2012) *The 1912 Stockholm Olympics: Essays on the Competitions, the People, the City.* Jefferson: McFarland.

6 Mega-crises and mega-events

Anticipated, unexpected and latent threats

Introduction

Commenting on the extended French state of emergency ahead of Euro 2016, then-Prime Minister Manuel Valls conceded that this period of exceptional state powers '[could] not be permanent, but for these big events . . . we have decided to prolong it' (quoted in *The Independent*, 2016). Initially, the French state of emergency was declared in the wake of the November 2015 Paris attacks (Fredette, 2017). Yet Valls' comments clearly point towards the connections between the politics of security, emergency, and the European Championships, which we address in this chapter. They also depict the wider dimensions of uncertainty that characterize modern-day sport mega-events like the Euros (see Lee Ludvigsen, 2022a). In the face of uncertainty, Valls' comments demonstrate how a prolonged state of emergency covering the 'big event' was considered a necessary action by some. Euro 2016 is not the only Euros edition that has been disrupted by external threats. Moreover, in the wider European context, the European Championships have played an important role in activating relationships between European security agencies in order to ensure information sharing and cooperation reflecting the politicization of security, models of European understanding and responses to threats (Tsoukala, 2009: 79–80, 118). As such, this chapter sets out to discuss the types of external threats or emergencies that have impacted the Euros between 2016 and 2024. Specifically, we address how these have been, or are, publicly responded to.

This chapter discusses three emergency typologies that have emerged with a specific intensity and disrupted or impacted the organization of the European Championships between 2016–2024. Our argument is that these typologies have been primarily characterized by *anticipation* (the terrorist threat before Euro 2016), *complete unexpectedness* (Covid-19 and Euro 2020) and *latency* (Euro 2024's environmental discourses). Importantly, whereas these threats remain co-existent and non-exhaustive, they are also

DOI: 10.4324/9781003359098-6

marked by a special intensity as they appear to be more pronounced than other threats ahead of specific mega-events. Drawing from documentary and media data and sentiment analysis, this chapter will contend that the Euros can be approached as one specific moment from which responses to *wider* emergencies and insecurities spring out. Yet, before pinpointing snapshots of the threats via the lenses of Euro 2016, 2020 and 2024, we begin with some theoretical considerations speaking to the nexus between emergency, security and uncertainty, as this will assist our understanding of how the Euros mirror and attend to the evolving security agenda.

Security, emergency and uncertainty

In the social and political sciences, the political management of and occasional overlaps between the concepts of 'security', 'crisis', 'risk' and 'emergency' have composed key themes in the work of influential scholars such as Beck (1992), Foucault (2007), Agamben (2005) and Bigo (2006). The concept of 'security' is fluid, evolving and often used to justify new exceptional practices (Bigo, 2006) or extraordinary measures (Buzan et al., 1998). However, whilst the traditional readings of 'security' were mainly focused on *national* security (Bigo, 2012), states and military power, the post-Cold War and post-9/11 timescapes have seen the emergence of new security threats.

Across Europe, numerous security issues and emergencies – borne out of internal and external events – collectively comprise the multifaceted European security agenda (Schroeder, 2013). Whilst this includes, perhaps most notably, the threat of transnational terrorism and crime, it is also possible to locate environmental issues (Brown and McLeman, 2009), health issues like pandemics (Elbe, 2018) and economic issues like recessions and food and job security on the twenty-first century security agenda as *threats* to international, national and individual security. Given that these co-existing threats are all characterized by levels of uncertainty, this highlights the complicated nature of states and institutions' pursuit of security.

Following Fussey and Coaffee (2011), the 'generalized' and 'externalized' risks influencing the management of security in more general contexts are the key drivers behind sport mega-events' security programmes. However, whilst scholars have examined the connection between sport mega-events and 'terrorism' (Fussey and Coaffee, 2011; Giulianotti and Klauser, 2012; Boyle and Haggerty, 2012), it is crucial to acknowledge that the types of threats that characterize specific mega-events differ in their intensity, as this chapter showcases. Hence, in such securitized milieus, managing and responding to emergencies and uncertainties has become a key dimension of modern mega-events like the Euros (Lee Ludvigsen, 2022a).

This poses questions of how exactly mega-event organizers and stake-holders deal with situations that are loaded with 'unknowns' *vis-a-vis* the potential damage or harm that may be caused (Adey et al., 2015; Beck, 1992). One tendency that is emphasized in the literature, however, is the precautionary thinking that has embedded itself in the securitization of mega-events (Boyle and Haggerty, 2012) and in distinct ways mirrors the increased significance of 'worst-case' thinking in the operational manage-ment of uncertainty (Clark, 2008).

Though, by following Beck (1992), the action of merely hypothesizing or contemplating 'worst-case' scenarios or potential emergencies provides no panacea for actually minimizing risks or threats, in spite of such episte-mological drawbacks in predicting the future, this has led to authorities or stakeholders increasingly *showcasing* that they have subscribed to a pre-cautionary logic (Boyle and Haggerty, 2012). This relates to the 'societal expectation' on leaders or experts to be in control (Clarke, 2008: 156). And so, one way of (at least) appearing to be in control relates to how the man-agement of uncertainty is *communicated* to the public (Boyle and Haggerty, 2012). Significantly, this renders public responses to security, threats and emergencies extremely relevant because they exemplify how (in)security is both framed, imagined and contested.

Whilst Boyle and Haggerty (2012) analyse the Olympics, Lee Ludvig-sen (2022a) finds that many of the similar security logics were embedded in Euro 2020's organization. Building on these insights, this chapter seeks to re-apply these analytical relations by using snapshots from Euro 2016, 2020 and 2024 to explore, more specifically, how different stakeholders publicly addressed three typologies of threats situated on the expanding security agenda and characterized by uncertainty and potential destructive-ness. We focus on the threats of terrorism, pandemics and environmental issues which provide insight into the diversity and changing *intensity* of emergencies that have impacted the tournaments (2016–2024). To reiterate, these three threat typologies are neither exhaustive nor mutually exclusive – and they are characterized by anticipation, unexpectedness and latency. Our main argument is that the responses to these threats underpin how the Euros now compose a specific site through which responses to more 'generalized' and 'externalized' (Fussey and Coaffee, 2011) emergencies – that fluctuate between being instant or pending – are formulated.

Anticipation: state of emergency at Euro 2016

Between 10 June and 10 July 2016, Euro 2016 was staged whilst the host country, France, was on a high alert following the terrorist attacks in Paris and Saint Denis on 13 November 2015. One of these attacks had targeted

Stade de France during a fixture between France and Germany, and in the aftermath of these tragic events, the French government activated a state of emergency. The state of emergency was initially meant to last for 12 days (Fredette, 2017), but was later extended five times and did not expire until November 2017 (Dück and Lucke, 2019), which meant that it influenced directly the housing of Euro 2016.

The declaration of a state of emergency – in the name of national security – is traditionally synonymous with enhanced state powers, which may translate into a suspension of civil liberties or restrictions on individuals' movement (Armitage, 2002). Fundamentally, it represents a temporary departure from 'normal' politics in a time of crisis or extraordinary uncertainty (see Agamben, 2005). This meant that, in France, the activated state of emergency provided authorities with the power to search private homes without warrants, and to stop public demonstrations or place individuals under house arrest if it was suspected that they would represent a threat to the public order (see Fredette, 2017). Thus, unsurprisingly, the need to secure France and Euro 2016 emerged as a central talking point before the tournament. Yet, with Euro 2016 being situated within a highly securitized climate – marked by the enhanced empowerment of French authorities – this raises questions of the discursive features speaking to the *anticipation* of terrorism that closely followed Euro 2016.

In April 2016, reports emerged maintaining that France sought to extend the state of emergency – due to expire on 26 May 2016 – so that it would cover Euro 2016 and the annual *Tour de France* cycling race (BBC, 2016a). By some, this proposal, subject to parliamentary approval, was unequivocally framed first in terms of 'security' and, second, in terms of allowing Euro 2016 to proceed in a celebratory manner. For example, as Valls commented: 'We must ensure full security [so that Euro 2016 can] be at the same time a celebration with full stadiums and full fan zones' (quoted in Sky Sports, 2016a). Discursively, an extended state of emergency was partly framed (and justified) in relation to Euro 2016 and, when the extended state of emergency was confirmed in late May 2016, Valls also stated that cancelling Euro 2016 was not a realistic option, noting that: 'Giving up on sporting events and cultural events is precisely to give in to the terrorist threat' (quoted in Sky Sports, 2016b). These quotes underline how the exceptional but also inherently precautionary security arrangements intended to secure Euro 2016 were framed as a necessary response to heightened threat levels, whilst also serving a purpose of showing that France would not give in to the threat or let it impede the tournament's spirit.

Similarly, in Euro 2016's build-up, then-French President Francois Hollande also insisted that the tournament would proceed as planned despite heightened security as he urged citizens to not let fears ruin the prospects of a 'European festival' (ESPN, 2016). Indeed, these examples underline how, before Euro 2016, a 'secure and festive tournament was perceived as a political message to terrorists and a proof that France remained France' (Divsasova, 2019: 261), hence the terms of promoting values of the state and democracy.

Whilst the discursive and performative aspects of security (e.g., in public discourses) are emphasized by securitization theorists as fundamental for the social construction of security threats and to justify extraordinary measures (see Buzan et al., 1998), it remains crucial to highlight here that the threat of terrorism was already highly securitized *before* Euro 2016. Rather, it can be argued that the tournament instead became a specific reference point through which securitizing discourses could be reinforced or emerge in the context of. The anticipated threat and Euro 2016's symbolic status consequently became central in the wider French response to terrorism threats, which influenced *both* the security arrangements of the tournament (Parent and Reutsch, 2020; see also BBC, 2016b, for a special report) as well as the wider French society which the prolonged period of exceptional state powers impacted.

Notwithstanding, even though the discourses that focused on extending the state of emergency for the purpose of secure Euro 2016 were predominantly framed in terms of the acute terrorist threat, Euro 2016 was also largely impacted by scenes of supporter violence across seven of its host cities involving supporters from various countries (Domeneghetti, 2020). However, as Divasova (2019) argues, the prospects of 'hooliganism' were also largely anticipated before the event by French authorities, although they were largely overshadowed by the urgent need to respond to the terrorist threat. This momentum meant that a controversial 'counter-hooligan' law passed in the French Parliament to little opposition, much due to the emergency politics that affected Euro 2016's build-up and delivery. Thus, in this chapter's context, this section demonstrates how the *anticipated* terrorism threat was responded to in France and how Euro 2016 became situated at the forefront of the wider emergency politics dominating the country in the post-2015 period.

Unexpectedness: Euro 2020 and the pandemic

Whereas the processes surrounding the one-year postponement of Euro 2020 are covered elsewhere (Lee Ludvigsen, 2022a, 2022b; Bond et al., 2022) we focus here on how the sudden and unexpected threat of Covid-19 was responded to in the case of Euro 2020. Whilst Euro 2020, as stated in Chapter 2, was meant to mark the competition's 60th anniversary and be staged across cities in 12 European countries in June and July 2020, the tournament was hugely impacted by an unprecedented and unexpected threat as the coronavirus spread across Europe and the world in the early days of 2020 and throughout the next year (Lee Ludvigsen, 2022a).

The pandemic and its potential impact on the tournament forced UEFA to – on 17 March 2020 – announce that they postponed Euro 2020 to a new set of dates in June/July 2021. This was a decision made that could be analysed in relation to public health and safety and, as Lee Ludvigsen (2022a) argues, the suddenness and unexpected nature of the pandemic threat was demonstrated by how a postponement was not considered a likely outcome by some stakeholders until late February 2020 and early March 2020, which was merely weeks before the postponement. As the global spread of Covid-19 continued to escalate, this forced European football leagues and the Euros into 'shut-down' within the space of one week (11–17th March 2020) (ibid.). It is possible to observe, through a sentiment analysis (see Figure 6.1) of tweets in English mentioning Euro 2020, that this unlikeness of outcome had only changed on the 12 March when it was announced by UEFA that key stakeholders were going to meet on 17 March to decide on the postponement. Until then, there was a positive sentiment permeating across tweets in terms of the tournament that was supposed to celebrate the 60th anniversary of the Euros across the whole continent.

Nevertheless, whilst both the key dates of 12 March and 17 March were on average negative days in terms of sentiment on Twitter, it was 26 March that was most negative as users retweeted a tweet by the Liberal Democrat party leader Sir Edward Davey MP, where both the postponement of Euro 2020 and Tokyo Olympic Games were conflated with risks associated with global economic disruptions and the ongoing Brexit talks (EdwardJDavey, 2020). In essence, whilst the pandemic was a much unprecedent health crisis, the ramifications were well anticipated in other areas such as economics and politics. Hence, as Beck (1992, 2010, 2016) argued, in the current cosmopolitan condition the interdependent nature of crisis causes everyone to experience it – *an* equal *distribution of bads* – whilst the catastrophic anticipations and its ubiquity representation in the different media forces conjoint actions that explode borders, be they of nation-states in terms of supra-national collaboration, or within nation-states in terms of distinct organizations and stakeholders.

When Euro 2020 eventually took place in the summer of 2021 – in 11 rather than 12 countries – the presence of crowds (and difficulties in maintaining social distancing) in stadiums and fan zones became a contentious issue that was considered a possible driver for Covid-19 transmission rates across the continent given the tournament's continental format and associated fan mobilities. These concerns were articulated by various external actors, including the World Health Organization and the German Interior

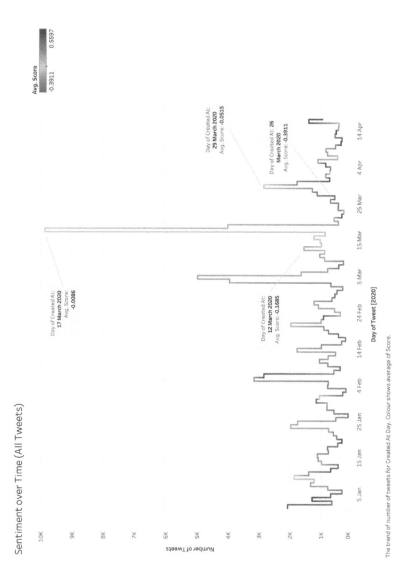

The trend of number of tweets for Created At Day. Colour shows average of Score.

Figure 6.1 Tweets Sentiment Analysis (Euro 2020's postponement)

Minister, Horst Seehofer, who called the decision to allow fans inside stadiums 'utterly irresponsible' despite UEFA's insistence that they were fully aligned with local health bodies' guidelines in each of the 11 host countries, but that local increases in case numbers could not be completely excluded (Reuters, 2021). As such, whilst sport's governing bodies framed their responses in terms of adherence to health guidance and scientific expertise (see Lee Ludvigsen, 2022b), it can simultaneously be argued that, in the context of the already discussed literature on mega-event security governance, the processes associated with the staging of Euro 2020 during a time of growing Covid-19 cases in Europe show not only how public responses centre around how security can be achieved (e.g., postponement, following health guidance), but how counter-discourses of concern and *insecurity* also spring up from mega-events countering the security-oriented responses.

Latency: environmental concerns in the Euro 2024 bid

In 2024, Germany will host the Euros. Undeniably, potential issues speaking to terrorism, supporter violence and infectious diseases (especially in the 'post-pandemic' era) are among those threats that the German organizers and authorities will have to contemplate. However, this section focuses on another type of emergency: One which, following Beck (1992, 2016), can be considered more *diffuse* and *pending* insofar as its consequences may be tempo-spatially unlimited and which is characterized by a longer latency period. As accurately illustrated by environmental problems, this means that more time is likely to pass (what can be called a 'latency period') between the 'initial event' and the hazardous outcomes (see Beck and Kropp, 2007).

In recent years, the 'improved scientific understanding of the risks of anthropogenic climate change has steadily pushed it to the top of the list of environmental threats to human security' (Brown and McLeman, 2009: 293). In accordance with wider international and European political and security agendas (Kelemen and Vogel, 2010; on environmental security, see Biswas, 2011) and warnings of ecological destruction and loss since the 1980s (Redclift, 2009), issues of sustainability and environmental issues and sustainability policies have for the last two decades become situated at the frontiers of sport mega-events (Ross and Orr, 2022).

This has intensified the need for sport mega-events to adopt various strategies in order to reduce their impact on climate change and for organizing committees to consider events' impacts on the natural environment (Ross and Orr, 2022) stemming from transport, waste, construction work and consumption (Horne, 2010). In this chapter's overarching context, environmental problems – although they substantially differ in nature from the discussed uncertainties from terrorism and infectious diseases – may be considered a security threat that is more latent but must be similarly responded to *institutionally* and *publicly*. Indeed, the destructiveness of this threat may intensify *after* the event.

Notably, the case of Euro 2024 underscores this. In the early bidding process, environmental concerns and sustainability were unsurprisingly among the key areas that bidders were required to pro-actively address by UEFA. For example, UEFA's (2017, Sector 3: 3) requirements for 2024 bidders state that one of the key challenges for the eventual Euro 2024 host(s) related to 'minimising the environmental footprint' of the tournament. This speaks to UEFA's ability to define, redefine or reinforce risks (see Eick, 2011) and, as Chapters 2 and 5 mentioned, aspiring host countries must guarantee to meet UEFA's requirements. And so, in terms of the environmental requirements UEFA set out consideration points for bidders, including the implementation of measures to 'minimise the impact of the event (in relation to energy, water, waste etc.)' (ibid.: 4) and leaving behind environment-related legacies such as lessons that can be shared within the circuits of mega-events (ibid.).

Germany successfully secured the Euro 2024 hosting rights in September 2018 (UEFA, 2018a). In terms of environmental aspects, UEFA's (2018b: 15) bid evaluations suggested that the German bid exceeded the related expectations, and by exploring the discourses in the German bid book, it is observed that the successful bid was repeatedly framed in terms of its potential impacts on environmental and climate protection. However, here it is also possible to draw a distinction between the bid's goals to address the latent threat *within* the tournament and *beyond* the tournament.

Concerning the former, this speaks to climate-friendly policies related to the actual staging of Euro 2024, including 'combi-tickets' (combined match and transport tickets to ensure climate-friendly travelling) or optimized energy use within stadiums, hotels and hospitality areas (DFB, n.d.: 45). Concerning the latter, this relates to *longer-term* precautionary responses to environmental problems that were embedded in the bid, resonating directly with those ideas of mega-event 'legacies' (Horne, 2010).

For instance, Euro 2024 was framed as an event that: 'will be used to launch countless projects and programmes to avoid and reduce possible negative environmental impacts of staging UEFA EURO 2024' (DFB, n.d.: 44). Moreover, the bid was also framed as a catalyst for new standards ahead of *future* events through its generation of: 'new benchmarks for subsequent tournaments and thus enhance the general environmental standards at large-scale events' (ibid.). Although these are selected examples, these discourses reveal how the environmental issues beyond Euro 2024's 'lifetime' were addressed *via* the event.

In this chapter's context, these precautionary measures addressing a latent environmental concern are important. Ultimately, they encapsulate how those largely uncontrollable issues that feature centrally on the expanding global security agenda in the twenty-first century, such as terrorism, infectious diseases and the environment (Biswas, 2011; Van Der Hen and Sun, 2021), are clearly on the mega-event host countries' radars and thus increasingly central within the organization and requirements of the Euros. Furthermore, in making a return to Boyle and Haggerty's (2012) work on the Olympic Games, we also see how, in the Euros' context, potential emergencies and emerging threats such as environmental problems must not only – as far as possible – be contemplated, but the responses to these emergencies must also be *publicly articulated* or *contested*. In line with Boyle and Haggerty, we observe that these discursive processes – be they through newspaper interviews, official statements, social media or bidding documents – remain central because they epitomize how those in charge of organizing the Euros, past and present, work to reassure the public that potentially damaging uncertainties can be managed or, at least, *are* being addressed.

Conclusion

This chapter demonstrated how external events and (potential) threats have impacted and continue to loom over the European Championships as the event circulates in between national contexts. Each edition is delivered amid dynamic climates characterized by uncertainty. Some of these emerge due to the Euros' status as an extraordinary event (Hagemann, 2010) drawing in mass crowds and global media attention (Chapters 3 and 4). But then, occasionally, the Euros are staged within and (re-)fuel pre-existing, exceptional circumstances.

Against this background, this chapter's purpose was twofold. In providing three snapshots or mini cases (set between Euro 2016 and 2024), the first goal was to outline the contours of three threat typologies. Second, we predominantly sought to examine how these were responded to in public communications and discourses and thereby how the relevant threat was framed, contested or imagined. Thus, this chapter identified three key typologies of threats that have affected or continue to affect the Euros. Whilst we again underline that these non-exhaustive threats *co-exist* ahead of most mega-events, we argue that these typologies fluctuate in their prominence ahead of specific tournaments and that were marked by *anticipation* (illustrated by Euro 2016's state of emergency), *unexpectedness* (illustrated by Euro 2020's Covid-19 postponement) and, finally, *latency* (illustrated by Euro 2024's environmental policies).

Taken together, these examples reinforce the idea that precautionary logics drive the attempts to secure mega-events (Boyle and Haggerty, 2012; Lee Ludvigsen, 2022a), and thus how more 'generalized' security discourses and imaginations are manifested in mega-events, as Lee Ludvigsen (2022a) has previously argued. Building upon this, we also argue that the responses to the three different threats underline how we can understand the Euros as a locus from which responses to wider materialized or pending emergencies are generated and formulated. For example, we observe how Euro 2016 was partly framed as *one* reason to prolong the state of emergency in France. Meanwhile, Euro 2020's crowds and the climate programmes in the German bid for Euro 2024 were also framed as having a temporospatial impact *beyond* the tournament and host cities themselves. Indeed, whilst this relates to existing ideas of European football as a 'testing ground' for security practices (Tsoukala, 2009; Lee Ludvigsen, 2022a), the argument we forward in this chapter remains important by itself because it speaks to how the Euros compose transient occasions that are framed and imagined in terms of the wider European and global provisions, pursuits and manifestations of security.

References

Adey P, Anderson B and Graham S (2015) Introduction: Governing emergencies: Beyond exceptionality. *Theory, Culture & Society* 32(2): 3–17.

Agamben G (2005) *State of Exception.* Chicago: University of Chicago Press.

Armitage J (2002) State of emergency: An introduction. *Theory, Culture & Society* 19(4): 27–38.

BBC (2016a) *France Seeks State of Emergency Extension for Euro 2016.* Available at: www.bbc.co.uk/news/world-europe-36089675 (accessed 08/2022).

BBC (2016b) *France Euro 2016: Hollande Warns Unions Against Disrupting Tournament.* Available at: www.bbc.co.uk/news/world-europe-36494702 (accessed 08/2022).

Beck U (1992) *Risk Society: Towards a New Modernity.* London: Sage.

Beck U (2010) *Cosmopolitan Vision.* Cambridge: Polity.

Beck U (2016) *The Metamorphosis of the World.* Cambridge: Polity.

Beck U and Kropp C (2007) Environmental risks and public perceptions. In: J Pretty et al. (eds.) *The Sage Handbook of Environment and Society.* Los Angeles: Sage, pp. 601–611.

Bigo D (2006) Globalized (in)security: The field and the ban-opticon. In: D Bigo and A Tsoukala (eds.) *Illiberal Practices of Liberal Regimes: The (In)security Games.* Paris: Editions L'Harmattan, pp. 5–49.

Bigo D (2012) Security, surveillance and democracy. In: D Lyon, KD Haggerty and K Ball (eds.) *Routledge Handbook of Surveillance Studies.* Abingdon: Routledge, pp. 277–284.

Biswas NR (2011) Is the environment a security threat? Environmental security beyond securitization. *International Affairs Review* 20(1): 1–22.

Bond A, Parnell D and Lee Ludvigsen JA (2022) Postponement of events. In: N Wise and K Maguire (eds.) *A Research Agenda for Event Impacts*. Cheltenham: Edward Elgar Publishing, pp. 193–202.

Boyle P and Haggerty KD (2012) Planning for the worst: Risk, uncertainty and the Olympic Games. *The British Journal of Sociology* 63(2): 241–259.

Brown O and McLeman R (2009) A recurring anarchy? The emergence of climate change as a threat to international peace and security. *Conflict, Security & Development* 9(3): 289–305.

Buzan B, Waever O and De Wilde J (1998) *Security: A New Framework for Analysis*. Boulder: Lynne Rienner.

Clarke L (2008) Thinking about worst-case thinking. *Sociological Inquiry* 78(2): 154–161.

DFD (n.d.) *United by Football. In the Heart of Europe. Sustainability Concept UEFA Euro 2024 Germany*. Available at: www.dfb.de/fileadmin/_dfbdam/178855-EURO_2024_Nachhaltigkeitskonzept.pdf (accessed 06/2022).

Divišová V (2019) Euro 2016 and its security legacy for football supporters: A conceptual blurring of hooligans and terrorists? *Soccer & Society* 20(5): 757–769.

Domeneghetti R (2020) Football hooliganism. In: R Steen, J Novick and H Richards (eds.) *Routledge Handbook of Sports Journalism*. London: Routledge.

Dück E and Lucke R (2019) Same old (Macro-) Securitization? A comparison of political reactions to major terrorist attacks in the United States and France. *Croatian International Relations Review* 25(84): 6–35.

EdwardJDavey (2020) [Twitter] 26 March. Available at: https://twitter.com/edward jdavey/status/1243095101804601344 (accessed 08/2022).

Eick V (2011) 'Secure our profits!' The FIFA in Germany 2006. In: C Bennett and K Haggerty (eds.) *Security Games. Surveillance and Control at Mega-Events*. New York: Routledge, pp. 87–102.

Elbe S (2018) *Pandemics, Pills, and Politics: Governing Global Health Security*. Baltimore: JHU Press.

ESPN (2016) *Euro 2016 Will Be a Success, We Can't Give in to Fear – Francois Hollande*. Available at: www.espn.co.uk/football/european-championship/story/2887131/euro-2016-will-be-a-success--we-cant-give-in-to-fear-francois-hol lande (accessed 08/2022).

Foucault M (2007) *Security, Territory, Population: Lectures at the College De France, 1977–78*. Basingstoke: Palgrave Macmillan.

Fredette J (2017) The French state of emergency. *Current History* 116(788): 101–106.

Fussey P and Coaffee J (2011) Olympic rings of steel: Constructing security for 2012 and beyond. In: C Bennett and KD Haggerty (eds.) *Security Games: Surveillance and Control at Mega-Events*. London: Routledge, pp. 36–54.

Giulianotti R and Klauser F (2012) Sport mega-events and 'terrorism': A critical analysis. *International Review for the Sociology of Sport* 47(3): 307–323.

Hagemann A (2010) From the stadium to the fan zone: Host cities in a state of emergency. *Soccer & Society* 11(6): 723–736.

Horne J (2010) Material and representational legacies of sports mega-events: The case of the UEFA EURO™ football championships from 1996 to 2008. *Soccer & Society* 11(6): 854–866.

The Independent (2016) *Euro 2016: France is Supposed to be in a State of Emergency – But You Wouldn't Know It.* Available at: www.independent.co.uk/sport/football/international/euro-2016-france-in-state-of-emergency-but-you-wouldn-t-know-it-fan-violence-paris-a7081431.html (accessed 06/2022).

Kelemen RD and Vogel D (2010) Trading places: The role of the United States and the European Union in international environmental politics. *Comparative Political Studies* 43(4): 427–456.

Lee Ludvigsen JA (2022a) *Sport Mega-Events, Security and COVID-19: Securing the Football World.* Oxon: Routledge.

Lee Ludvigsen JA (2022b) When 'the show' cannot go on: An investigation into sports mega-events and responses during the pandemic crisis. *International Review for the Sociology of Sport* 57(4): 497–514.

Parent M and Reutsch A (2020) *Managing Major Sports Events.* London: Routledge.

Redclift M (2009) The environment and carbon dependence: Landscapes of sustainability and materiality. *Current Sociology* 57(3): 369–387.

Reuters (2021) *German Minister Chides 'Irresponsible' UEFA Over Euro 2020 Crowds.* Available at: www.reuters.com/world/europe/german-minister-slams-uefas-decision-fuller-stadiums-2021-07-01/ (accessed 08/2022).

Ross WJ and Orr M (2022) Predicting climate impacts to the Olympic Games and FIFA Men's World Cups from 2022 to 2032. *Sport in Society* 25(4): 867–888.

Schroeder U (2013) *The Organization of European Security Governance: Internal and External Security in Transition.* London and New York: Routledge.

Sky Sports (2016a) *France Government Call for State of Emergency Extension at Euro 2016.* Available at: www.skysports.com/football/news/19692/10251162/france-government-calling-for-state-of-emergency-during-euro-2016 (accessed 06/2022).

Sky Sports (2016b) *France Extend State of Emergency to Cover Euro 2016 and Tour de France.* Available at: www.skysports.com/football/news/19692/10287839/france-extend-state-of-emergency-to-cover-euro-2016-and-tour-de-france (accessed 06/2022).

Tsoukala A (2009) *Football Hooliganism in Europe: Security and Civil Liberties in the Balance.* Basingstoke: Palgrave Macmillan.

UEFA (2017) *UEFA Euro 2024: Tournament Requirements.* Available at: www.uefa.com/multimediafiles/download/officialdocument/uefaorg/regulations/02/46/30/61/2463061_download.pdf (accessed 06/2022).

UEFA (2018a) *Germany to Host UEFA Euro 2024.* Available at: www.uefa.com/insideuefa/about-uefa/news/0249-0f8-40dc5e1-2ebf8efacf63-1000--germany-to-host-uefa-euro-2024/ (accessed 06/2022).

UEFA (2018b) *UEFA Euro 2024: Evaluation Report, UEFA: Nyon.* www.uefa.com/MultimediaFiles/Download/OfficialDocument/competitions/General/02/57/28/19/2572819_DOWNLOAD.pdf (accessed 06/2022).

Van der Ven H and Sun Y (2021) Varieties of crises: Comparing the politics of COVID-19 and climate change. *Global Environmental Politics* 21(1): 13–22.

7   Conclusion

Towards a sociology of the Euros

In an epoch where Europe is facing various external and internal challenges (Bauman, 2016), this book's central thesis is that the European Championships in men's football has further reinforced its position as a central, popular cultural reference point in Europe and can be understood as an expression for changing societies across the continent. Moreover, whilst the Euros are contested only by *European* nations (Chapter 1), the repercussions of each competition and their organizations and mediations are felt across the world.

Whilst wider transformations have directly transformed the Euros, the mega-event itself and its commercial, media-related and political developments have simultaneously generated social changes speaking to consumption, the pursuit and organization of the competition, and its broadcasting and remediated presence on (new) digital media. Therefore, with reference to this book's intellectual goal, a sociology of the European Championships is one that utilizes its coalescent status as a *mega-event*, a *media event* and a *political event* as entrance points to understand how the specific tournaments and the mega-event (as a whole) impact social relations, communication, and consumption in mediated and physical spaces, and further appreciates how these changes are facilitated by the interactions between consumers, media networks, political actors and sport's governing bodies, most notably UEFA.

However, this book argues that the European Championships not only reflects wider changes in European and world societies but also act as a locomotive driving forward those changes, and as a laboratory for influential actors situated across sport, politics, media and the corporate world. The Euros, we maintain, can be seen as a driver for new media practices, digital interactions, shared experiences and images, collaborative efforts between (host) countries, security agendas and symbolic visions of Europe. Such an argument rests on this book's exploratory approach to diverse social issues including the intensified commercialism and mediation of sport (Chapter

DOI: 10.4324/9781003359098-7

2), changing digital media and consumption patterns (Chapters 3 and 4), mega-event bidding, housing practices and political opposition (Chapter 5) and finally, the politics of security and emergencies (Chapter 6).

As sketched out in Chapter 1, the principal purpose of this book related to the production of a sociological analysis of the contemporary social issues, digital and political trends associated with what is the third-biggest sport mega-event in the world and requires systematic and serious sociological inquiry. One of the motivations behind this book related to the fact that the Euros – when positioned next to the (Summer) Olympics and the FIFA World Cup – have been assigned substantially less research. Whilst important encyclopaedic texts have been written that develop sociologies or political histories of the Olympics and the World Cup (Boykoff, 2016; Chadwick et al., 2022; Roche, 2000, 2017), a contemporary sociology of the European Championships has hitherto remained under-developed, although this does not mean that academics have not seen its sociological value (Chapters 1 and 2). Whilst this underlines the identified research gap this book bridges, the importance and timeliness of this book is underpinned by the (ever-)expanding European festival, which has grown immensely over the last 60 years in terms of its size, global reach, commercial activities and its social, spatial and cultural impacts on cities, individuals and groups across Europe and beyond.

As such, we reiterate that – from a sociological perspective – the Euros composes a cauldron of social issues which, crucially, is of unique relevance for sociologists of politics, culture, consumption and the digital world as well as sociologists of sport.

In this text, which has blended traditional 'desk-based' approaches with the methodological opportunities provided by research agendas and advances in digital sociology (see Chapter 1), we have remained conceptually and theoretically open-minded, flexible and experimental. Important to acknowledge, this has been a deliberate move because we believed it would work to enhance the book's ability to showcase the diversity of insights within the library of the social sciences that can be borrowed, called upon or synthesized to improve our understanding of the Euros. In a way, we sought to zoom *in* and *out* of particular European Championships and the wider Euros phenomenon, look at them through different academic traditions such as political science, media and business studies and particularly sociology, ultimately seeking to provide a more *complete* view of this important mega-event. Indeed, we openly acknowledge the limitations of our exploratory approach and the fact that we have chosen the topics and cases ourselves. Moreover, we have not covered *all* editions of the European Championships as we have mostly confined ourselves to the twenty-first century. Nevertheless, the arguments this book advances – in tandem with its rich material – should be considered to matter sociologically for three main reasons.

First, this book's arguments matter because they capture a key pillar of 'Europe', regardless of how one defines 'Europe' (Chapter 1). Whilst academics have already discussed whether European football may – or may not – promote European identities or boost Europeanization processes (Manzenreiter and Spitaler, 2010; Millward, 2009), our discussions of bidding/hosting alliances (Chapter 5) and Twitter interactions (Chapter 3) tie into these debates and collectively illustrate the opportunities, but also the *obstacles* for interactions on state, regional and individual levels as initiated by the football competition. For Delanty (2002: 351), '[p]opular music, sport, the Euro [currency], are possible expressions of this new kind of Europe, but it is one that is largely shaped by consumer capitalism'. Thus, whilst we see some developments that may indicate European integration (for example, joint ventures between EU and non-EU co-hosts or bid alliances and security-related collaborations), our discussion of media practices reveals that the *nation-state* still remains the primary reference for the media, whilst linguistics factors (limiting interaction on social media) similarly appear as obstacles to processes of a coherent Europeanization. Therefore, the importance of this book speaks to its renewed emphasis on how the Euros possess a *dual role* as a site of socio-cultural integration *and* the maintenance of lines of cultural division (see Manzenreiter and Spitaler, 2010) or nationalist perceptual frames (Law, 2014).

Second, this book remains unique in how it bridges insights from digital sociology and political sociology and resultantly avoids a perceived *silofication* of knowledge. Thereby, this research can be considered to partake in wider sociological projects speaking to engagement (and experimentation) of digital approaches to sociological aspects (Selwyn, 2019; Lupton, 2014), whilst also examining how 'the digital' intersects with political sociology's orientation towards how political actors play distinct roles in shaping the social structures such as the economy, nationality and cultures (Faulks, 2000). In a nutshell, ideas relating to social change – deemed central in both the digital and political sociologies – feed into this book's overarching focus on and unique application to sport. In that respect, this book has empirically documented and theoretically expanded on how – within the European Championships' context – a digitally networked ecosystem is now deeply embedded in the tournament's wider political economy which, again, relies upon sport/media alliances (Hachleitner and Manzenreiter, 2010) and is maintained through integrations, dependencies and political interactions between (sub-)political actors that possess varying degrees of power and interests. Most prominently, this involves nations (host countries/ bidders), corporations (sponsors, broadcasters) and the 'global governor' of UEFA (event owner) (Włoch, 2013). As we show, the interactions that take place around socially and politically constructed mega-events ultimately have enormous implications on social relations, digital cultures and public spaces across Europe and beyond (Chapter 4).

Third, as much as this is a text about the European Championships, it is also a social study of sport mega-events. One of the rationales behind this book was to explore issues emanating in the broader context of mega-events that had been assigned less discussion in the European Championships' setting. Importantly, it is not our intention to downplay the differences between the Olympics, the FIFA World Cup and the Euros. However, although the Euros, for example, remain 'much more limited in scope' than the Olympics, the tournaments' development has been moulded by many similar economic, cultural and political trends (Hachleitner and Manzenreiter, 2010: 844). We maintain that this book represents an important addition to the contemporary scholarship on mega-events, which in itself remains sociologically important as the study of essentially neoliberal and socio-urban enterprises that migrate between places and attract 'diverse forms of opposition, criticism and complaint' (Giulianotti et al., 2015: 116). Taken together, this means that this monograph, under a wider sociological umbrella, offers a contribution to (i) understandings of European popular culture, (ii) digital and political sociological research programmes and (iii) the sections of the sociology of sport concerned with mega-events and European football.

Mega-events in times of continual change

Here, throughout our chapters and in our other academic work, we agree with Roche's (2017: 42) proposition holding that '[m]ega-events have always tended to reflect and mark the times in which they are produced'. However, this simultaneously implies that, as time goes on and societies change, so do mega-events as essentially social products change. Mega-events are in – and represent – continual change. To account for this, this section reflects on the possibilities for future research on the European Championships in football and other football mega-events. Significantly, we argue that a sociology of the Euros remains an ongoing project for which this book acts as a trampoline.

First, one of the main shortcomings of this book relates to how we focus throughout on the men's Euros. We have therefore provided little substantial analysis of the women's Euros, and we have not discussed other international tournaments governed by UEFA, such as Under-21 tournaments or the Beach Soccer or Futsal Euros. This is explained by space restrictions which placed certain boundaries on the book's scope. And to be sure, this does not reflect the scholarly importance of these mentioned events. In a time where the interest in women's football has grown consistently (Petty and Pope, 2019), and against the backdrop of the recent women's Euro 2022 in England, we would argue that future work should explore many of the same trends that we have explored in the context of the women's game. This includes, but is not confined to, changing media practices, digitalization processes, event bidding and emergency politics. Yet, researchers may – as Beissel et al. (2022) did in the context of the 2023 Women's World Cup – explore whether specific hosting visions integrate the promotion of gender equality and social changes more broadly within the event-specific contexts.

Second, and beyond Europe, we encourage researchers to increasingly explore other continental football mega-events, including Copa America, Africa Cup of Nations and the Asian Cup which, like the Euros, are bound to raise a host of sociological questions. Whilst we contended that the Euros have been under-researched in comparison to the Olympics and the World Cup, similar arguments may undoubtedly be forwarded in relation to these abovementioned competitions. Here, we would also highlight the importance of incorporating non-Western perspectives which would not only benefit development of mega-event studies, but would also reinforce wider projects speaking to the renewal of critical social theory (see Delanty, 2009).

Third, from a methodological perspective, we invite scholars to blend the use of 'traditional' social research methods with those approaches that are offered by advances within the digital world and digital sociology (Chapters 3 and 4). With the current platformization of society and its wider impact on the cultural industries (van Dijck et al., 2018; Poell et al., 2022), it is important for researchers to be attuned to what happens *in* different media, and specifically be attuned to the ever-evolving data politics (see Srnicek, 2017) that directly impact the ability to study specific platforms through their APIs. Yet, whilst some platforms such as Twitter and YouTube currently have academic programs for accessing user-generated data through their APIs (Twitter, 2022; YouTube, 2022), other platforms like TikTok or Instagram remain more secret, requiring researchers to adapt their practices to fully capture mega-events' digital parametres and reach.

Finally, the physical and digital fandom practices related to the European Championships warrant further research. This relates to fandom in 'traditional' spaces, such as stadiums, fan zones, host cities or pubs as well as 'online' spaces where fandom increasingly is performed and acquires meanings. Based on this book and our earlier work (e.g., Petersen-Wagner, 2017, 2019; Lee Ludvigsen, 2019), it is for example scope to explore the connection between cosmopolitanism, transnational solidarities and fandom practices of the Euros (see also Millward, 2010), whereas further research is needed to continually understand how the Euros may be a catalyst for collective identities (Roche, 1998), changing fan cultures, nationalistic or continent-wide European rituals (cf. King, 2003). Other research questions relate to how the experience of a European Championships provides fans – aided by platforms like TikTok, YouTube, Twitch or Twitter – the possibility to engage in new fan communities and invent new fandom traditions afforded by second screen use and social media, allowing for the practices of what we may call '*supporting-together-apart*' and '*supporting-apart-together*'.

***

Whilst these directions relate to the persistent development of the sociology of the European Championships or a sociological re-imagination of ever-changing mega-events, these are not pathways directed solely towards sociologists of sport. The expansion of knowledge on the third-largest mega-event in the world, we argue, largely depends on committed efforts from scholars situated in different fields, whom we hereby invite to contribute further towards this project.

It is commonly stated that Europe is currently experiencing a turbulent and uncertain time (Bauman, 2016; Giddens, 2014). Over the last fifteen years, this is *inter alia* illustrated by impactful developments such as the Eurozone crisis, humanitarian crises, Brexit and its aftermath, the rise of populist parties, the 2022 Russian invasion of Ukraine and the post-Covid 're-opening' of societies and subsequent 're-activation' of mobilities. These may all be considered 'critical moments' in Europe (Hutter and Kriesi, 2019), which ultimately will require further attention by researchers in the future *vis-a-vis* their relation to European football and sport.

Under these conditions of uncertainty, this leads us to ask what the positions of European football, and more specifically the Euros, are within this continuum. King (2010: 899), writing shortly after the 2008 financial crisis, argued that '[a]s a public ritual, [European football] is embedded into wider institutional and political realities of which it is a conscious reflection and manifestation', and that 'football may be able to provide a perspicuous view of Europe's future'. As our book's key arguments illustrate, there are several reasons that King's outlook could be maintained. For example, as a dialogue partner UEFA maintains close ties with institutions like the EU and the Council of Europe (Garcia et al., 2011; UEFA, n.d.). UEFA has also reflected wider responses to crises such as Covid-19 (Lee Ludvigsen, 2022) and the Russian invasion of Ukraine (UEFA, 2022). Indeed, as Garcia et al. (2011) maintain, UEFA's central governance position means that it not merely generates Europeanizing dynamics from EU decisions; it also remains a force of transformation in itself. For such transformations, we argue, the Euros represent an integral tool.

Whilst we suggest that in the 2020s and 2030s, the Euros are likely to tell us more about citizens' digital consumption habits and preferences, European countries' desire to cooperate to host tournaments and organizations' adaption to a changing sport and media landscape, this mega-event is also likely to reflect and manifest (cf. King, 2010) wider European security (Lee Ludvigsen, 2022) and geopolitical developments, nationalist ideologies, cultural division or discrimination (*The Guardian*, 2021) and questions about data ownership and privacy. Naturally, *exactly* how the Euros will shape Europe's path(s) in the future remains to be seen, but what is for certain is that this mega-event is inseparable from the broader contexts in which it takes place and is produced, consumed and pursued.

It is partly for this reason that this volume's main argument, contending that the Euros represent a key cultural reference point and an expression for European societies, also remains subject to revision and development as time passes and the continent undergoes new transformations that trigger critical junctures.

References

Bauman Z (2016) *Strangers at our Door?* Cambridge: Polity Press.

Beissel A, Postlethwaite V and Grainger A (2022) 'Winning the women's world cup': Gender, branding, and the Australia/New Zealand as one 2023 social media strategy for the FIFA Women's World Cup 2023™. *Sport in Society* 25(4): 768–798.

Boykoff J (2016) *Power Games: A Political History of the Olympics*. London/New York: Verso Books.

Chadwick S, Widdop P, Anagnostopoulos C and Parnell D (eds.) (2022) *The Business of the FIFA World Cup*. London: Routledge.

Delanty G (2002) Models of European identity: Reconciling universalism and particularism. *Perspectives on European Politics and Society* 3(3): 345–359.

Delanty G (2009) *The Cosmopolitan Imagination: The Renewal of Critical Social Theory*. Cambridge: Cambridge University Press.

Faulks K (2000) *Political Sociology: A Critical Introduction*. New York: NYU Press.

Garcia B, Niemann A and Grant W (2011) Conclusion. In: A Niemann, B Garcia and W Grant (eds.) *The Transformation of European Football: Towards the Europeanisation of the National Game*. Manchester: Manchester University Press, pp. 239–261.

Giddens A (2014) *Turbulent and Mighty Continent: What Future for Europe?* Cambridge: Polity Press.

Giulianotti R, Armstrong G, Hales G and Hobbs D (2015) Sport mega-events and public opposition: A sociological study of the London 2012 Olympics. *Journal of Sport and Social Issues* 39(2): 99–119.

The Guardian (2021) *Uefa Receives Report on Homophobic Banner at Hungary v Portugal Match*. Available at: www.theguardian.com/football/2021/jun/16/uefa-receive-report-on-homophobic-banner-at-hungary-v-portugal-match.

Hachleitner B and Manzenreiter W (2010) The EURO 2008 bonanza: Mega-events, economic pretensions and the sports – media business alliance. *Soccer & Society* 11(6): 843–853.

Hutter S and Kriesi H (2019) Politicizing Europe in times of crisis. *Journal of European Public Policy* 26(7): 996–1017.

King A (2003) *The European Ritual: Football in the New Europe*. London: Routledge.

King A (2010) After the crunch: A new era for the beautiful game in Europe? *Soccer & Society* 11(6): 880–891.

Law A (2014) Playing with tension: National charisma and disgrace at Euro 2012. *Soccer & Society* 15(2): 203–221.

Lee Ludvigsen JA (2019) Transnational fan reactions to transnational trends: Norwegian Liverpool supporters, 'authenticity' and 'filthy-rich' club owners. *Soccer & Society* 20(6): 872–890.

Lee Ludvigsen JA (2022) *Sport Mega-Events, Security and COVID-19: Securing the Football World*. Oxon: Routledge.

Lupton D (2014) *Digital Sociology*. London: Routledge.

Manzenreiter W and Spitaler G (2010) Governance, citizenship and the new European football championships: The European spectacle. *Soccer & Society* 11(6): 695–708.

Millward P (2009) *Getting into Europe: Identification, Prejudice and Politics in English Football Culture*. Saarbrucken: VDM Verlag.

Millward P (2010) The limits to cosmopolitanism: English football fans at Euro 2008. In: D Burdsey (ed.) *Race, Ethnicity and Football: Persisting Debates and Emergent Issues*. London: Routledge, pp. 163–174.

Petersen-Wagner R (2017) The football supporter in a cosmopolitan epoch. *Journal of Sport and Social Issues* 41(2): 133–150.

Petersen-Wagner R (2019) Between old and new traditions: Transnational solidarities and the love for Liverpool FC. In: S Lawrence and G Crawford (eds.) *Digital Football Cultures: Fandom, Identities and Resistance*. London: Routledge, pp. 47–65.

Petty K and Pope S (2019) A new age for media coverage of women's sport? An analysis of English media coverage of the 2015 FIFA Women's World Cup. *Sociology* 53(3): 486–502.

Poell T, Nieborg D and Duffy BE (2022) *Platforms and Cultural Production*. Cambridge: Polity Press.

Roche M (eds.) (1998) *Sport, Popular Culture and Identity*. Aachen: Meyer & Meyer.

Roche M (2000) *Mega-Events and Modernity: Olympics and Expos in the Growth of Global Culture*. London: Routledge.

Roche M (2017) *Mega-Events and Social Change: Spectacle, Legacy and Public Culture*. Manchester: Manchester University Press.

Selwyn N (2019) *What is Digital Sociology?*. Cambridge: John Wiley & Sons.

Srnicek N (2017) *Platform Capitalism*. Cambridge: Polity Press.

Twitter (2022) *Academic Research Access*. Available at: https://developer.twitter.com/en/products/twitter-api/academic-research (accessed 13/05/2022).

UEFA (2022) *UEFA Decisions for Upcoming Competitions Relating to the Ongoing Suspension of Russian National Teams and Clubs*. Available at: www.uefa.com/insideuefa/mediaservices/mediareleases/news/0275-150c9887cacb-882c686f407f-1000--uefa-decisions-for-upcoming-competitions-relating-to-the-ongoin/.

UEFA (n.d.) *UEFA and the European Institutions*. Available at: www.uefa.com/insideuefa/stakeholders/european-union/.

van Dijck J, Poell T and de Waal M (2018) *The Platform Society: Public Values in a Connective World*. Oxford: Oxford University Press.

Włoch R (2013) UEFA as a new agent of global governance: A case study of relations between UEFA and the Polish government against the background of the UEFA EURO 2012. *Journal of Sport and Social Issues* 37(3): 297–311.

YouTube (2022) *YouTube Researcher Program*. Available at: https://research.youtube (accessed 22/07/2022).

Appendix

This appendix contains key information about the data that was analysed for Chapter 4.

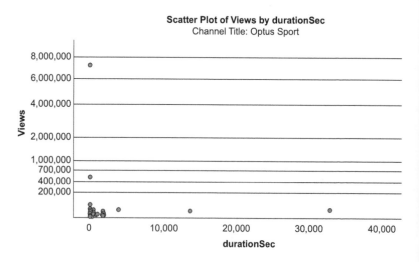

Figure A.1 Scatter Plot (Optus Sport [Australia])

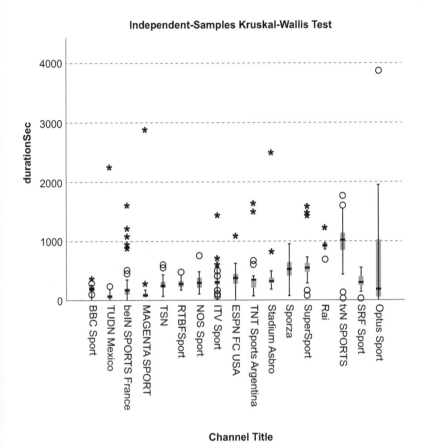

Figure A.2 Duration in seconds

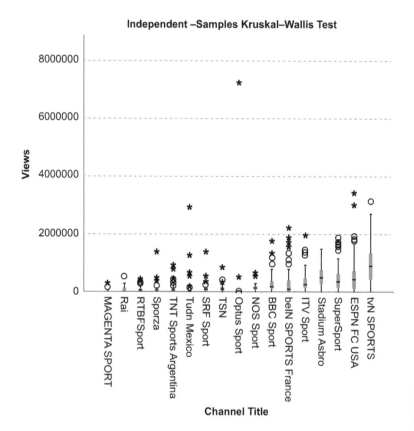

Figure A.3 Views

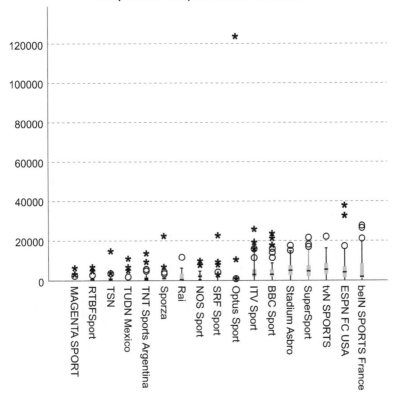

Figure A.4 Likes

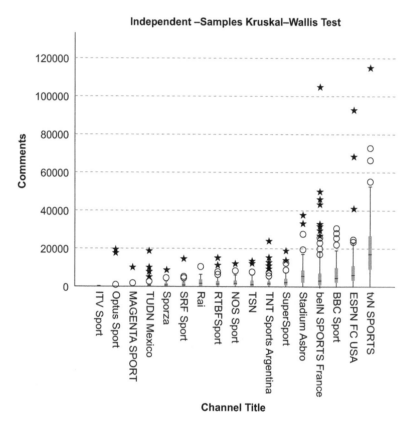

Figure A.5 Comments

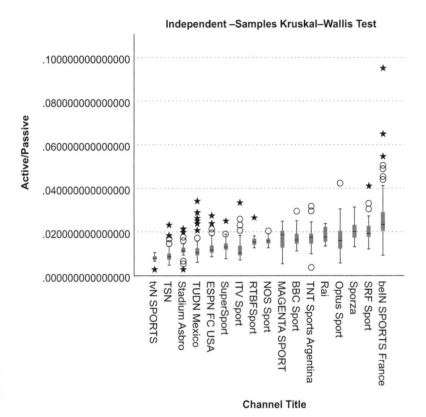

Figure A.6 Active/Passive

Table A.1 Descriptive Statistics

Descriptive Statistics

Channel Title		N	Minimum	Maximum	Mean	Std. Deviation
BBC Sport	durationSec	76	58	383	205.83	56.956
	Views	76	10209	1,760,298	311,189.25	335,234.502
	Likes	76	140	23,604	4,209.96	4,610.946
	Comments	76	15	4,491	875.43	1,056.111
	Active/Passive	76	.0113	.0297	.0173	.0034
	Valid N (listwise)	76				
beIN SPORTS France	durationSec	217	6	1,612	193.56	176.905
	Views	217	3,193	2,219,796	279,690.03	367,199.507
	Likes	217	91	27,773	5,028.93	5,876.582
	Comments	217	1	1.0496	631.47	1,059.732
	Active/Passive	217	.0094	.0952	.0256	.0091
	Valid N (listwise)	217				
ESPN FC USA	durationSec	75	17	1,094	364.59	174.238
	Views	75	7,293	3,428,007	609,693.49	658,838.990
	Likes	75	122	38,098	6,024.99	6,735.281
	Comments	75	40	9,314	1,002.07	1,408.262
	Active/Passive	75	.0085	.0276	.0132	.0040
	Valid N (listwise)	75				
ITV Sport	durationSec	99	70	1,447	328.53	156.510
	Views	99	21,377	1,957,247	361,721.14	331,106.201
	Likes	99	221	25,739	4,450.84	4,540.022
	Comments	99	0	0	.00	.000
	Active/Passive	99	.0074	.0520	.0123	.0059
	Valid N (listwise)	99				

	N	Minimum	Maximum	Mean	Std. Deviation
MAGENTA SPORT					
durationSec	52	66	2,878	163.71	386.638
Views	52	7,241	313,422	55,942.27	67,494.845
Likes	52	134	6,183	821.37	1,078.642
Comments	52	4	1,012	64.69	141.415
Active/Passive	52	.0054	.0249	.0172	.0046
Valid N (listwise)	52				
NOS Sport					
durationSec	51	121	760	310.25	119.295
Views	51	38,583	677,311	165,649.65	113,937.396
Likes	51	615	10,020	2,413.67	1,647.166
Comments	51	45	1,202	254.92	238.607
Active/Passive	51	.0129	.0209	.0162	.0016
Valid N (listwise)	51				
Optus Sport					
durationSec	81	12	32,510	1,137.27	3,887.259
Views	81	929	7,251,733	102,545.72	806,347.946
Likes	81	8	123,860	1,755.36	13,787.410
Comments	81	0	1,975	62.25	292.147
Active/Passive	81	.0059	.0425	.0171	.0065
Valid N (listwise)	81				
Rai					
durationSec	7	698	1,232	937.14	159.114
Views	7	3,003	54,6743	126,146.00	213,914.229
Likes	7	41	11,846	2,705.43	4,651.130
Comments	7	2	1,066	257.00	429.406
Active/Passive	7	.0137	.0239	.0188	.0042
Valid N (listwise)	7				
RTBFSport					
durationSec	34	180	496	295.09	69.139
Views	34	8273	46,7941	109,232.97	108,890.277
Likes	34	212	6,519	1,435.41	1,469.934
Comments	34	9	1,501	254.38	345.889
Active/Passive	34	.0126	.0267	.0157	.0024
Valid N (listwise)	34				

(Continued)

Table A.1 (Continued)

Descriptive Statistics

Channel Title		N	Minimum	Maximum	Mean	Std. Deviation
Sporza	durationSec	56	86	955	532.14	179.274
	Views	56	9,524	1,384,645	113,133.91	202,622.946
	Likes	56	211	22,418	1,846.93	3,129.040
	Comments	56	5	897	148.39	178.772
	Active/Passive	56	.0132	.0316	.0205	.0039
	Valid N (listwise)	56				
SRF Sport	durationSec	72	31	11,756	1,797.31	3,305.611
	Views	72	32,779	1,394,309	128,913.33	173,804.436
	Likes	72	675	22,683	2,341.49	2,894.812
	Comments	72	7	1454	148.68	198.705
	Active/Passive	72	.0122	.0412	.0205	.0047
	Valid N (listwise)	72				
Stadium Astro	durationSec	61	191	2489	380.92	289.695
	Views	61	8,459	1,495,163	555,977.57	412,096.304
	Likes	61	53	17,561	5,976.34	4,772.233
	Comments	61	3	3,794	783.57	781.770
	Active/Passive	61	.0030	.0214	.0119	.0027
	Valid N (listwise)	61				
SuperSport	durationSec	64	87	1,592	584.61	289.311
	Views	64	2,995	1,885,786	494,336.38	470,735.696
	Likes	64	37	21,680	5,864.23	5,178.675
	Comments	64	7	1,906	349.28	375.610
	Active/Passive	64	.0081	.0251	.0137	.0026
	Valid N (listwise)	64				

TNT Sports Argentina	durationSec	58	82	1,641	352.50	256.280
	Views	58	2,561	92,6207	129,567.91	179,428.484
	Likes	58	57	13,739	1,700.45	2,362.775
	Comments	58	6	2,398	316.09	443.087
	Active/Passive	58	.0039	.0319	.0178	.0047
	Valid N (listwise)	58				
TSN	durationSec	60	79	605	268.35	101.978
	Views	60	5,998	866,975	139,660.35	143,684.094
	Likes	60	32	14,891	1,196.00	2,000.500
	Comments	60	7	1,358	238.97	300.454
	Active/Passive	60	.0049	.0234	.0094	.0033
	Valid N (listwise)	60				
TUDN Mexico	durationSec	72	24	2,258	112.15	261.431
	Views	72	2,876	2,943,650	139,366.04	400,715.378
	Likes	72	35	31,581	1,336.07	4,115.986
	Comments	72	1	1,891	142.93	312.841
	Active/Passive	72	.0061	.0343	.0121	.0051
	Valid N (listwise)	72				
tvN SPORTS	durationSec	54	31	1,769	1,001.50	320.636
	Views	54	7265	3,156,547	1,071,627.17	785,524.098
	Likes	54	48	22,181	6,595.70	4,912.024
	Comments	54	5	11,517	2,261.61	2,133.723
	Active/Passive	54	.0029	.0107	.0082	.0012
	Valid N (listwise)	54				

Table A.2 Correlations

Correlations			durationSec	Views	Likes
Channel Title					
BBC Sport	Spearman's rho	Views			
		Correlation Coefficient	.586**		
		Sig. (2-tailed)	.000		
		N	76		
		Likes			
		Correlation Coefficient	.568**	.982**	
		Sig. (2-tailed)	.000	.000	
		N	76	76	
		Comments			
		Correlation Coefficient	.466**	.910**	.881**
		Sig. (2-tailed)	.000	.000	.000
		N	76	76	76
beIN SPORTS France	Spearman's rho	Views			
		Correlation Coefficient	.029		
		Sig. (2-tailed)	.672		
		N	217		
		Likes			
		Correlation Coefficient	.041	.990**	
		Sig. (2-tailed)	.550	.000	
		N	217	217	
		Comments			
		Correlation Coefficient	−.061	.902**	.892**
		Sig. (2-tailed)	.372	.000	.000
		N	217	217	217
ESPN FC USA	Spearman's rho	Views			
		Correlation Coefficient	.674**		
		Sig. (2-tailed)	.000		
		N	75		
		Likes			
		Correlation Coefficient	.662**	.991**	
		Sig. (2-tailed)	.000	.000	
		N	75	75	
		Comments			
		Correlation Coefficient	.723**	.915**	.912**
		Sig. (2-tailed)	.000	.000	.000
		N	75	75	75

ITV Sport	Spearman's rho	Views	Correlation Coefficient	−.015		
			Sig. (2-tailed)	.880		
			N	99		
		Likes	Correlation Coefficient	−.038	.943**	
			Sig. (2-tailed)	.712	.000	
			N	99	99	
		Comments	Correlation Coefficient	.	.	.
			Sig. (2-tailed)	.	.	.
			N	99	99	99
MAGENTA SPORT	Spearman's rho	Views	Correlation Coefficient	.669**	.944**	.890**
			Sig. (2-tailed)	.000	.000	.000
			N	52	52	52
		Likes	Correlation Coefficient	.659**	.889**	
			Sig. (2-tailed)	.000	.000	
			N	52	52	
		Comments	Correlation Coefficient	.638**		
			Sig. (2-tailed)	.000		
			N	52		
NOS Sport	Spearman's rho	Views	Correlation Coefficient	.582**	.965**	.785**
			Sig. (2-tailed)	.000	.000	.000
			N	51	51	51
		Likes	Correlation Coefficient	.506**	.828**	
			Sig. (2-tailed)	.000	.000	
			N	51	51	
		Comments	Correlation Coefficient	.436**		
			Sig. (2-tailed)	.001		
			N	51		

(Continued)

Table A.2 (Continued)

Correlations

Channel Title				durationSec	Views	Likes
Optus Sport	Spearman's rho	Views	Correlation Coefficient	-.012		
			Sig. (2-tailed)	.915		
			N	81		
		Likes	Correlation Coefficient	-.124	.903**	
			Sig. (2-tailed)	.271	.000	
			N	81	81	
		Comments	Correlation Coefficient	-.218	.564**	.542**
			Sig. (2-tailed)	.051	.000	.000
			N	81	81	81
Rai	Spearman's rho	Views	Correlation Coefficient	-.036		
			Sig. (2-tailed)	.939		
			N	7		
		Likes	Correlation Coefficient	.036	.893**	
			Sig. (2-tailed)	.939	.007	
			N	7	7	
		Comments	Correlation Coefficient	-.072	.991**	.937**
			Sig. (2-tailed)	.878	.000	.002
			N	7	7	7
RTBFSport	Spearman's rho	Views	Correlation Coefficient	.620**		
			Sig. (2-tailed)	.000		
			N	34		
		Likes	Correlation Coefficient	.578**	.986**	
			Sig. (2-tailed)	.000	.000	
			N	34	34	
		Comments	Correlation Coefficient	.445**	.835**	.773**
			Sig. (2-tailed)	.008	.000	.000
			N	34	34	34

Sporza	Spearman's rho	Views	Correlation Coefficient	.413**		
			Sig. (2-tailed)	.002		
			N	56		
		Likes	Correlation Coefficient	.285*	.962**	
			Sig. (2-tailed)	.033	.000	
			N	56	56	
		Comments	Correlation Coefficient	.398**	.781**	.789**
			Sig. (2-tailed)	.002	.000	.000
			N	56	56	56
SRF Sport	Spearman's rho	Views	Correlation Coefficient	.432**		
			Sig. (2-tailed)	.000		
			N	72		
		Likes	Correlation Coefficient	.336**	.915**	
			Sig. (2-tailed)	.004	.000	
			N	72	72	
		Comments	Correlation Coefficient	.127	.737**	.700**
			Sig. (2-tailed)	.286	.000	.000
			N	72	72	72
Stadium Astro	Spearman's rho	Views	Correlation Coefficient	.057		
			Sig. (2-tailed)	.665		
			N	61		
		Likes	Correlation Coefficient	.062	.990**	
			Sig. (2-tailed)	.635	.000	
			N	61	61	
		Comments	Correlation Coefficient	−.033	.918**	.918**
			Sig. (2-tailed)	.799	.000	.000
			N	61	61	61

(Continued)

Table A.2 (Continued)

Correlations

Channel Title			durationSec	Views	Likes
SuperSport	Spearman's rho	Views	Correlation Coefficient	.236		
			Sig. (2-tailed)	.061		
			N	64		
		Likes	Correlation Coefficient	.198	.988**	
			Sig. (2-tailed)	.117	.000	
			N	64	64	
		Comments	Correlation Coefficient	.285*	.957**	.946**
			Sig. (2-tailed)	.023	.000	.000
			N	64	64	64
TNT Sports Argentina	Spearman's rho	Views	Correlation Coefficient	.193		
			Sig. (2-tailed)	.146		
			N	58		
		Likes	Correlation Coefficient	.108	.948**	
			Sig. (2-tailed)	.418	.000	
			N	58	58	
		Comments	Correlation Coefficient	.073	.907**	.948**
			Sig. (2-tailed)	.585	.000	.000
			N	58	58	58
TSN	Spearman's rho	Views	Correlation Coefficient	.534**		
			Sig. (2-tailed)	.000		
			N	60		
		Likes	Correlation Coefficient	.416**	.967**	
			Sig. (2-tailed)	.001	.000	
			N	60	60	
		Comments	Correlation Coefficient	.381**	.905**	.899**
			Sig. (2-tailed)	.003	.000	.000
			N	60	60	60

TUDN Mexico	Spearman's rho	Views	Correlation Coefficient	.673**		
			Sig. (2-tailed)	.000		
			N	72		
		Likes	Correlation Coefficient	.675**	.952**	
			Sig. (2-tailed)	.000	.000	
			N	72	72	
		Comments	Correlation Coefficient	.720**	.906**	.902**
			Sig. (2-tailed)	.000	.000	.000
			N	72	72	72
tvN SPORTS	Spearman's rho	Views	Correlation Coefficient	.557**		
			Sig. (2-tailed)	.000		
			N	54		
		Likes	Correlation Coefficient	.569**	.988**	
			Sig. (2-tailed)	.000	.000	
			N	54	54	
		Comments	Correlation Coefficient	.571**	.952**	.952**
			Sig. (2-tailed)	.000	.000	.000
			N	54	54	54

Table A.3 Non-parametric tests

Hypothesis Test Summary

	Null Hypothesis	Test	Sig.[a,b]	Decision
1	The distribution of durationSec is the same across categories of Channel Title.	Independent-Samples Kruskal-Wallis Test	.000	Reject the null hypothesis.
2	The distribution of Views is the same across categories of Channel Title.	Independent-Samples Kruskal-Wallis Test	.000	Reject the null hypothesis.
3	The distribution of Likes is the same across categories of Channel Title.	Independent-Samples Kruskal-Wallis Test	.000	Reject the null hypothesis.
4	The distribution of Comments is the same across categories of Channel Title.	Independent-Samples Kruskal-Wallis Test	.000	Reject the null hypothesis.
5	The distribution of Active/Passive is the same across categories of Channel Title.	Independent-Samples Kruskal-Wallis Test	.000	Reject the null hypothesis.

a. The significance level is .050.

b. Asymptotic significance is displayed.

Table A.4 Non-parametric test active/passive (non-significant)

Pairwise Comparisons of Channels (non-significant)

Sample 1-Sample 2	Test Statistic	Std. Error	Std. Test Statistic	Sig.	Adj. Sig.[a]
tvN SPORTS-TSN	86.113	64.410	1.337	.181	1.000
TSN-TUDN Mexico	−152.336	60.023	−2.538	.011	1.000
TSN-ITV Sport	155.916	56.180	2.775	.006	.750
TSN-Stadium Astro	175.017	62.435	2.803	.005	.688
TUDN Mexico-ITV Sport	3.580	53.185	.067	.946	1.000
TUDN Mexico-Stadium Astro	22.681	59.754	.380	.704	1.000
TUDN Mexico-ESPN FC USA	90.574	56.655	1.599	.110	1.000
TUDN Mexico-SuperSport	134.790	58.991	2.285	.022	1.000
TUDN Mexico-Rai	441.252	135.948	3.246	.001	.159
ITV Sport-Stadium Astro	−19.101	55.892	−.342	.733	1.000
ITV Sport-ESPN FC USA	86.994	52.565	1.655	.098	1.000
ITV Sport-SuperSport	−131.210	55.076	−2.382	.017	1.000
ITV Sport-Rai	−437.672	134.295	−3.259	.001	.152
Stadium Astro-ESPN FC USA	67.893	59.204	1.147	.251	1.000
Stadium Astro-SuperSport	−112.109	61.443	−1.825	.068	1.000
Stadium Astro-RTBFSport	240.882	73.491	3.278	.001	.142
Stadium Astro-Rai	418.571	137.030	3.055	.002	.306
ESPN FC USA-SuperSport	−44.216	58.433	−.757	.449	1.000
ESPN FC USA-RTBFSport	−172.989	70.993	−2.437	.015	1.000
ESPN FC USA-Rai	−350.678	135.707	−2.584	.010	1.000
SuperSport-RTBFSport	128.773	72.871	1.767	.077	1.000
SuperSport-NOS Sport	170.636	64.454	2.647	.008	1.000
SuperSport-Optus Sport	171.113	57.428	2.980	.003	.393
SuperSport-MAGENTA SPORT	215.025	64.108	3.354	.001	.108
SuperSport-Rai	306.462	136.699	2.242	.025	1.000
RTBFSport-NOS Sport	41.863	76.025	.551	.582	1.000
RTBFSport-Optus Sport	42.340	70.168	.603	.546	1.000
RTBFSport-MAGENTA SPORT	86.252	75.732	1.139	.255	1.000
RTBFSport-BBC Sport	98.736	70.847	1.394	.163	1.000
RTBFSport-TNT Sports Argentina	−112.290	74.168	−1.514	.130	1.000
RTBFSport-Rai	−177.689	142.520	−1.247	.212	1.000
NOS Sport-Optus Sport	−.477	61.381	−.008	.994	1.000
NOS Sport-MAGENTA SPORT	44.390	67.671	.656	.512	1.000
NOS Sport-BBC Sport	56.873	62.156	.915	.360	1.000

(*Continued*)

Table A.4 (Continued)

Pairwise Comparisons of Channels (non-significant)

Sample 1-Sample 2	Test Statistic	Std. Error	Std. Test Statistic	Sig.	Adj. Sig.[a]
NOS Sport-TNT Sports Argentina	−70.427	65.916	−1.068	.285	1.000
NOS Sport-Rai	−135.826	138.406	−.981	.326	1.000
NOS Sport-Sporza	−224.201	66.464	−3.373	.001	.101
Optus Sport-MAGENTA SPORT	43.912	61.018	.720	.472	1.000
Optus Sport-BBC Sport	56.396	54.837	1.028	.304	1.000
Optus Sport-TNT Sports Argentina	−69.950	59.064	−1.184	.236	1.000
Optus Sport-Rai	−135.349	135.277	−1.001	.317	1.000
MAGENTA SPORT-BBC Sport	12.484	61.797	.202	.840	1.000
MAGENTA SPORT-TNT Sports Argentina	−26.038	65.577	−.397	.691	1.000
MAGENTA SPORT-Rai	−91.437	138.245	−.661	.508	1.000
MAGENTA SPORT-SRF Sport	−169.838	62.491	−2.718	.007	.894
MAGENTA SPORT-Sporza	−179.812	66.129	−2.719	.007	.890
BBC Sport-TNT Sports Argentina	−13.554	59.869	−.226	.821	1.000
BBC Sport-Rai	−78.953	135.630	−.582	.560	1.000
BBC Sport-SRF Sport	−157.354	56.472	−2.786	.005	.725
BBC Sport-Sporza	−167.328	60.473	−2.767	.006	.769
TNT Sports Argentina-Rai	65.399	137.394	.476	.634	1.000
TNT Sports Argentina-SRF Sport	143.800	60.585	2.374	.018	1.000
TNT Sports Argentina-Sporza	153.774	64.331	2.390	.017	1.000
Rai-SRF Sport	−78.401	135.948	−.577	.564	1.000
Rai-Sporza	−88.375	137.658	−.642	.521	1.000
Rai-beIN SPORTS France	−213.461	131.862	−1.619	.105	1.000
SRF Sport-Sporza	−9.974	61.181	−.163	.870	1.000
SRF Sport-beIN SPORTS France	−135.060	46.701	−2.892	.004	.521
Sporza-beIN SPORTS France	−125.086	51.467	−2.430	.015	1.000

Each row tests the null hypothesis that the Sample 1 and Sample 2 distributions are the same.
Asymptotic significances (2-sided tests) are displayed. The significance level is .050.

a. Significance values have been adjusted by the Bonferroni correction for multiple tests.

Index

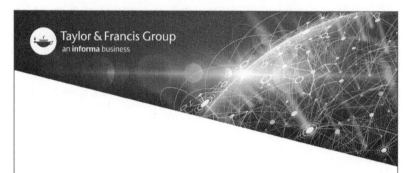